HOTSPOTS
SRI LAN

G000038360

Written by Debbie Stowe, updated Katerina Roberts
Original photography by Vasile Szakacs

Published by Thomas Cook Publishing
A division of Thomas Cook Tour Operations Limited.
Company Registration no. 3772199 England
The Thomas Cook Business Park, Unit 9, Coningsby Road,
Peterborough PE3 8SB, United Kingdom
Email: books@thomascook.com, Tel: + 44 (0) 1733 416477
www.thomascookpublishing.com

Produced by Cambridge Publishing Management Limited
Burr Elm Court, Main Street, Caldecote CB23 7NU

ISBN: 978-1-84848-101-5

First edition © 2007 Thomas Cook Publishing
This second edition © 2009
Text © Thomas Cook Publishing,
Maps © Thomas Cook Publishing/PCGraphics (UK) Limited

Series Editor: Adam Royal
Production/DTP: Steven Collins

Printed and bound in Spain by GraphyCems

Cover photography Alamy/PCL

CONTENTS

WHAT'S IN YOUR GUIDEBOOK?

Independent authors Impartial up-to-date information from our travel experts who meticulously source local knowledge.

Experience Thomas Cook's 165 years in the travel industry and guidebook publishing enriches every word with expertise you can trust.

Travel know-how Thomas Cook has thousands of staff working around the globe, all living and breathing travel.

Editors Travel-publishing professionals, pulling everything together to craft a perfect blend of words, pictures, maps and design.

You, the traveller We deliver a practical, no-nonsense approach to information, geared to how you really use it.

● *The enormous Buddha statue outside Weherahena Temple*

INTRODUCTION
Getting to know Sri Lanka

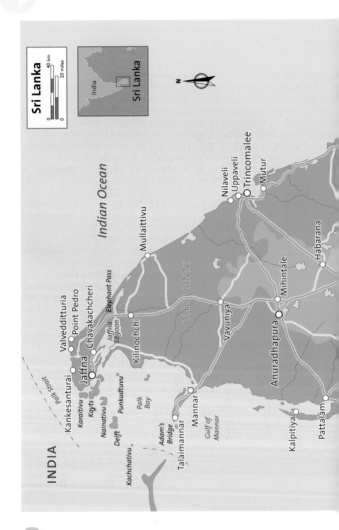

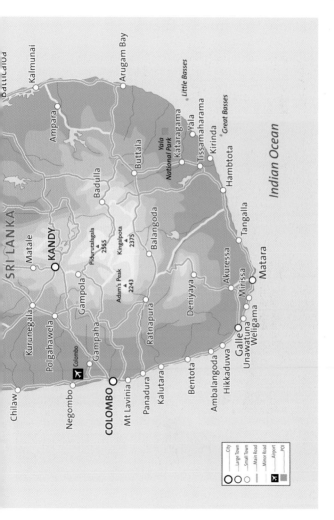

Getting to know Sri Lanka

The place explorer Marco Polo called the finest island of its size is often likened to a pearl, or teardrop falling down from India, and the romance of the comparisons is fully justified under closer inspection. Sri Lanka's changing names evoke its delights. Ceylon recalls the delicate pleasure

⬥ *Dancing is intrinsic to Sri Lankan culture*

of the island's most famous export: tea. Serendib, the country's old Arabic moniker, gave us the English word serendipity. That's certainly appropriate for this gem of a country, by far overshadowed by its large northern neighbour, India, but with a charm, friendliness and intimacy that only a small island can boast.

Sri Lankans have not had life easy. Over the ages their homeland has been beset by troubles, not least the tsunami that devastated a great deal of the coast in 2004. But it's testament to the optimism of its people that they have gone out and rebuilt their towns and livelihoods with fortitude, and seeing the smiles that greet you at every juncture it can be hard to imagine that tragedy ever touched this place. You're likely to reach the conclusion that an unfriendly Sri Lankan is a contradiction in terms.

Awaiting you in Sri Lanka is an incredible diversity of attractions, far more than a small island can usually muster. Most obviously there are the beaches – stretches of sand of an improbable beauty rarely seen outside holiday brochures. Thankfully, the resorts have escaped the commercialisation and development of comparable resorts such as Goa, and retain an untouched charm, which you can often enjoy almost entirely alone. On top of that there is the lush hill country, with its neatly verdant tea plantations, cool mountainous regions and an abundance of wildlife showcased in impressive national parks, the figurehead of which is probably the elephant, so venerated by Buddhists.

The national religion and its manifestations will also leave an imprint on your memory, from wonderful and unexpected little temples that crop up by the road or in villages, and orange-clad young monks, to the enormous Buddhas that sit sentinel overlooking larger sites. Sri Lanka's colourful culture, expressed through devotion, dance, markets and ancient medicine, makes the country far more than just a place to catch some rays on a golden stretch of sand. Most tourists might go for the beaches, but as the island's Arabic name promises, you may be blessed with serendipity and find that there are many more pleasant surprises to discover.

THE BEST OF SRI LANKA

TOP 10 ATTRACTIONS

- **Ayurveda Pavilions** Ayurveda is the holistic Eastern system of promoting well-being and prolonging life, practised throughout Sri Lanka and India (see page 26).

- **Adam's Peak** Shrouded in mist and mystery, the footprint shape at the mountain summit is said to belong to the Buddha. Energetic travellers can plant their own footprints on the pilgrim trail (see pages 81–2).

- **Eating out in Colombo** Sri Lanka's pleasant lack of commercialisation doesn't mean there's nowhere to get a decent meal. The capital boasts a complete range of top-quality eateries (see pages 21–2).

- **Unawatuna beach** This sleepy fishing village is popular with the not-so-sleepy; a favourite among independent travellers for its chilled-out nightlife (see page 47).

- **Bazaars in Colombo's Pettah district** Chaotic, colourful and convivial, Colombo's markets and bazaars showcase the country's retail therapy at its best – and it's all at bargain prices (see page 19).

- **Dutch villas in Galle** Step from Asia back into 17th-century Europe in Galle, whose luxury manor houses and cobbled labyrinthine lanes exude colonial charm (see page 57).

- **Temple of the Tooth, Kandy** The extraordinary deities, ornate gold and carvings, and spirituality of Sri Lanka's most sacred shrine leave an impression on even the most ardent atheist (see page 77).

- **Elephant and leopard-spotting at Yala National Park** Against a stunning landscape, Yala's magnificent leopards top the bill, while its elephants live up to their Latin name: *Elephas maximus* (see pages 87–8).

- **Watersports at Hikkaduwa** While adrenaline junkies tire themselves out with jet-skiing, surfing and diving, the more romantically inclined can get their thrills from a serene river safari (see pages 61–4).

- **Mirissa beach** Palm-fringed, pristine sands, postcard-perfect – it's difficult to describe beautiful Mirissa beach without resorting to holiday brochure clichés (see page 41).

⬇ *The lush greenery of the central province of Sri Lanka*

SYMBOLS KEY
The following symbols are used throughout this book:

ⓐ address ⓣ telephone ⓕ fax ⓦ website address ⓔ email
ⓛ opening times ⓝ public transport ⓘ important

The following symbols are used on the maps:

ℹ️	information office	◯	city
✉️	post office	◯	large town
🛍️	shopping	○	small town
✈️	airport	◾	POI (point of interest)
➕	hospital	═	motorway
🛡️	police station	—	main road
🚌	bus station	—	minor road
🚆	railway station	—	railway
✝️	church	Ⓝ	public transport
☪	mosque		

❶ numbers denote featured cafés, restaurants & evening venues

RESTAURANT CATEGORIES
The symbol after the name of each restaurant listed in this guide
indicates the price of a typical three-course meal without drinks
for one person:
£ = under R800   ££ = R800–1,400   £££ = over R1,400

◗ *Captivating tropical beaches of Sri Lanka*

RESORTS
Places under the sun

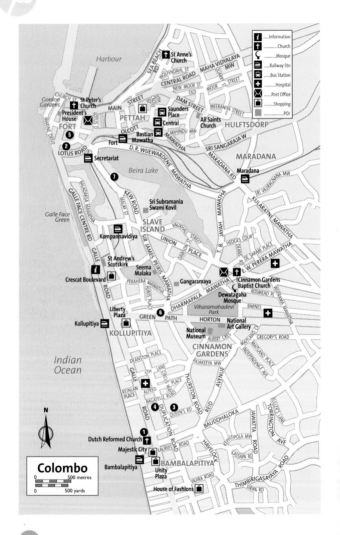

Colombo

i	Information
✝	Church
☾	Mosque
⛟	Railway Stn
🚌	Bus Station
✚	Hospital
✉	Post Office
🛍	Shopping
■	POI

Harbour

St Anne's Church

CHURCH ST.
Gordon Gardens
St Peter's Church
President's House
FORT
PETTAH
Saunders Place
Central
All Saints Church
HULFTSDORP
Olcott
Bastian Mawatha
Fort
Secretariat
MARADANA
Beira Lake
Maradana
Kew Road
Sri Subramania Swami Kovil
Galle Face Green
SLAVE ISLAND
Kompannavidiya
St Andrew's Scotskirk
Seema Malaka
Gangaramaya
Crescat Boulevard
Cinnamon Gardens Baptist Church
Dewatagaha Mosque
Viharamahadevi Park
Liberty Plaza
HORTON
National Art Gallery
Kollupitiya
KOLLUPITIYA
National Museum
CINNAMON GARDENS
Indian Ocean
DEANSTON PLACE
Dutch Reformed Church
Majestic City
Bambalapitiya
BAMBALAPITIYA
Unity Plaza
House of Fashions

N

Colombo
0   500 metres
0   500 yards

Colombo

As a contrast to many of the beach resorts, Sri Lanka's commercial capital could not get starker: where they are laid-back, it is hectic; and where they are quiet, it is noisy with traffic, trade and horns; where they are undeveloped, it is a bustling and built-up metropolis. But the comparison is not entirely to Colombo's detriment. In its favour, it has many cultural highlights, plus the sophisticated restaurant scene of a capital, with chic eateries that wouldn't disgrace themselves in any large European city. It's also the best place for shopping, with a range of malls and department stores stocking both Eastern and Western clothes and all manner of other merchandise, not forgetting the city's vibrant bazaar culture. Of course, Colombo contains all the juxtapositions of many big Asian cities: one minute you'll be passing a dreamy colonial

LIFE AFTER THE TSUNAMI

When the Indian Ocean tsunami struck on Boxing Day 2004, Sri Lanka's south and west coasts – home to the majority of its tourist industry – were badly hit. With international aid and the efforts of many voluntary organizations and individuals a Tsunami Warning System is now in place and recovery work is 98 per cent complete. Many hotels have been rebuilt or completely refurbished to international standards and businesses have reopened bringing employment to those who lost their livelihoods. Housing, schools, health centres and community projects are well-established bringing help to the affected towns and public transport was replaced, including the re-introduction in 2008 of the Colombo Fort to Matara train, *Queen of the Sea*, which made an historic journey, four years after killer waves damaged it and claimed over 1000 lives. Whatever resort you visit, you'll receive a genuine welcome and in your own way will be contributing to helping the local people to get their lives and business back on track.

mansion, the next your driver will be avoiding the cattle ambling along in the street.

If you've been travelling elsewhere in the region, Colombo may not even seem particularly extreme. It's cleaner, quieter and more peaceful than Delhi, for example, and there is far less obvious evidence of poverty, so it's nothing like as trying a city to spend time in as the Indian capital. And despite the obvious challenges for the Sri Lankans living there, they seldom suffer from the alienation and irritability common to big city-dwellers – you're always likely to be met with a smile, even from the armed guards who stand sentinel at checkpoints. The visible security in Colombo can at first be slightly intimidating to visitors not used to seeing guns on the street, but it soon becomes just part of the scenery, and the officers sometimes even offer to pose for a holiday snap!

Orientation poses some problems for the first-time visitor. The city is divided up into districts, numbered 1–15. Unfortunately, the numbers were not allocated on an obvious geographical basis, and are likely to be little help when you're trying to find your way around. Expect to be further puzzled by the street names: many of the colonial-era originals have been binned in favour of Sinhalese replacements. Not only are the original names more commonly known and used, but the inconsistency in local spellings of the new names also adds to the bewilderment. Starting from the north, the main quarters are Fort (Colombo 1), right by the Indian Ocean, home to the president's palace, and slightly further inland Pettah (Colombo 11), the market district. Moving south, by the water is Galle Face Green, a popular spot for romantic and family seaside promenades and swimming, and just inside is Slave Island (Colombo 2), which, rather confusingly, is not an island, but is bordered by Beira Lake. Moving down the coastline you come to posh Kollupitiya (Colombo 3), home to some upmarket shops and embassies, and inland from there is the trendy Cinnamon Gardens (Colombo 7), which includes a clutch of national museums and mansions, and to the north Viharamahadevi Park.

BEACHES

The commercial capital is not as blessed with beaches as much as the rest of the island, but that doesn't mean that if you base yourself here for a few days, sand, swimming and sunbathing are out of the question. Galle Face Green has a 2-km (¼-mile) stretch of sand, a few metres below the popular promenade. It's an urban beach, so don't go expecting the immaculate white sands of Mirissa or Polhena, but it's very popular with Sri Lankans. It has a pleasant, Sunday afternoon sort of atmosphere, with families and couples strolling along the walkway. The water is often full of groups of friends and local children swimming, and informal games of football or cricket often spring up, reinforcing the leisurely atmosphere. Another, less welcome denizen of the area is the Colombo conman, usually a respectable-looking old gentleman who will often spin an extended story about a deserving charity he's involved with. Be wary of such approaches.

THINGS TO SEE & DO

Dewatagaha Mosque

Divided into separate sections for men and women, the 200-plus-year-old mosque is chiefly celebrated for containing the tomb of Sheikh Usman Voliyullah. Prayer sessions, which are open to visitors, take place on Monday, Tuesday, Wednesday and Thursday around sunset and on Thursday at 21.00–22.00. If he's there, the friendly mosque manager will probably give you a tour.

ⓐ 12 Baptist Chapel Road, Colombo 7 ❶ (011) 268 3906, 078 524 9539
🕒 04.30–22.00

Gangaramaya

A large, quirky and fascinating temple, Gangaramaya is one of the city's most sacred spaces. The resident elephant and fish pond are just two of the noteworthy features of the site, which has plenty of intriguing nooks and crannies for exploration. Ornately-painted ceilings and Buddha statues lend the place charm and atmosphere, as does the library – a gloriously old-fashioned room that sometimes hosts lessons for local children. Another highlight is the museum, comprising two rooms that resemble a cross between an antiquated warehouse and a grandmother's living room. Inside the first is a delightfully random mishmash of old statues, pictures, books, gems, tusks, clocks, old chairs, cushions, fans and radios. There are even a few cars. The second room, for which there is a small entrance fee, holds more religious paraphernalia; some serious, some kitschy. While music plays, a monk may show you a 2,500-year-old fragment of Buddha bone. Meditation classes are held on Mondays from 06.00–07.00.

ⓐ 61 Sri Jinarathana Road, Colombo 2 ⓣ (011) 232 3038 ⓕ (011) 243 9508 ⓔ gt@gangaramaya.com ⓛ 08.00–20.00 ❶ Admission fee for museum

National Art Gallery
One large room of high-quality, 20th-century Sri Lankan art.
ⓐ Ananda Kumaraswamy Mawatha ⓣ (011) 269 3965
ⓛ 09.00–17.00 Sat–Thur

🔺 *The Colombo National Museum was founded in 1877*

National Museum

Charting the development of the island from prehistory to colonial times, the highlights of this large museum are probably the quirky collection of traditional masks and the Kandyan kings' finery. Information boards give the background and trivia.

ⓐ Marcus Fernando Mawatha ⓣ (011) 269 4767 ⓕ (011) 269 2092
ⓔ nmdep@slt.lk ⓛ 09.00–17.00 Sat–Thur, closed Fri and public holidays
ⓘ Admission fee

Pettah district

Colombo's market district is the uncovered Sri Lankan equivalent of Istanbul's Grand Bazaar: a bustling maze of interconnected streets, each one devoted to a particular type of merchandise. Tourists are usually most keen on the textiles of 3rd Cross and Keyzer Streets, the vegetables and spices of 5th Cross Street, the Ayurveda wares on Gabo Street, and Sea Street's gold jewellery. Even if you're not buying, the weaving porters, Tamil and Muslim presence, crammed stalls, competing music and smells of the stall snacks give Pettah a distinctive vibrancy and enjoyable chaos.

ⓐ East of Fort ⓛ Hours vary, most stalls and shops close on Sun

Seema Malaka

Designed by Geoffrey Bawa, Sri Lanka's top architect, the Seema Malaka temple seems to float on Beira Lake. It's the only temple in the country that eschewed tradition in design, putting simplicity over kitsch. The effect is modern yet mystical. Entrance is free but a donation is appreciated.

ⓐ Beira Lake, Colombo 2

Sri Siva Subramania Swami Kovil

Tall and striking Hindu temple whose ornate frontage is a mosaic of figures and faces of extraordinary detail. It's only open to the public for a couple of hours a day for *pujas* (religious rituals), but the lions, deities and numerous other intricate characters carved into the façade merit a visit.

ⓐ Kew Road, Slave Island ⓛ Approx. 08.00–09.00 & 17.00–18.00

Viharamahadevi Park

The city's largest open space is a delightful green area, beloved of young families and couples trying to get a few moments of privacy in a secluded area. Chief among the highlights is a big gold Buddha statue, but you can also enjoy a lake, fountain, open-air theatre, aquarium, jogging track and bandstand. The neat gardens are dotted with benches if you need a rest from the heat, and refreshment is provided care of the pineapple *wallahs* (people seemingly born to do a certain task). It's a great place to stop if you're travelling with children –

🔵 *The Seema Malaka temple – simple and non-traditional design*

there's climbing apparatus and from time to time a small fairground is in operation. Old-fashioned, slightly cheesy entertainment is on hand in the form of horse-and-cart rides.

ⓐ Horton Place

TAKING A BREAK

Bars & cafés
Barefoot Café ££ ❶ Set in the charming garden of a shop and art gallery, this homely café serves a refreshingly unusual selection of light meals and snacks. It's particularly proud of its fresh lime juice and calamari pasta, plus its chocolate cake, which it describes as 'positively wicked'. ⓐ 704 Galle Road, Colombo 3 ❶ (011) 255 3075 ⓦ www.barefoot.lk/Gallery-Cafe.htm ⓛ early–19.00

Café 64 ££ ❷ This café and garden terrace, situated by the hotel lobby, serves delicious pastries, sandwiches, cake, handmade chocolates, sweets, Italian coffee and fresh juices, and claims to be the only pastry shop in Colombo that serves beer and ice cream. ⓐ Hotel Galadari, 64 Lotus Road, Colombo 1 ❶ (011) 254 4544 ⓦ www.galadarihotel.com ⓛ 07.00–24.00

AFTER DARK

Restaurants
Cricket Club Café ££ ❸ A rare example of a theme restaurant that actually feels authentic rather than tacky, Cricket Club Café, with its cricket shirts and country flags, will delight the homesick and infuriate independent backpackers. The food is Western standards, from soups, salads and wraps to pastas, burgers, pies and other meat and veggie mains. Dish names, such as 'Beefie's Bolognese' and 'Khan's kebabs' seem to have been chosen for alliteration rather than culinary connection, but are tasty nevertheless. ⓐ 34 Queens Road, Colombo 3 ❶ (011) 250 1384 ⓛ 11.00–23.00

Thambapanni ££ ❹ Part restaurant and part art gallery, the food at this cosy eatery features both pure Sri Lankan and European fare with an emphasis on seafood. There's seating both inside and outside. ⓐ 496/1 Duplication Road, Colombo 3 ❶ (011) 250 0615, 072 211 8276 ❶ (011) 259 4496

Curry Leaf £££ ❺ Atmospheric, open-air restaurant in the Hilton's beautifully landscaped gardens or under a thatched roof. The buffet offers a costly but reliable introduction to traditional Sri Lankan fare such as chilli crab, *thosai* and *kottu*. Other Hilton eateries do international, Japanese, Cantonese and Szechuan and Italian food. ⓐ The Hilton, 2 Sir Chittampalam A Gardiner Mw, Colombo 2 ❶ (011) 254 4644 ⓔ colombo@hilton.com ❶ 19.00–24.00

Mango Tree £££ ❻ Sleek, stylish and air-conditioned, the Mango Tree combines smart, low-key décor with zesty Asian food, including Indian, Basmati and lots of veggie options. If you're only there to drink, the outside terrace with its Japanese-style pond is a pleasant place to sit. ⓐ 82 Dharmapala Mw, Colombo 3 ❶ (011) 587 9790 ⓦ www.themangotree.net ⓔ info@themangotree.net ❶ 12.00–14.45, 19.00–22.45 ❶ Credit cards accepted

Royal Thai £££ ❼ Sumptuously decorated top-of-the-range Thai restaurant. Tom yam, pad thai, curries and chicken pandan leaves are a few of the choices, all of which look and taste superb. ⓐ Trans-Asia Hotel, 115 Sir Chittampalam A Gardiner Mw, Colombo 2 ❶ (011) 249 1000 ext. 1945 ⓦ www.transasiahotel.com ❶ 12.00–14.30, 19.00–23.00

Exotic Sri Siva Subramania Swami Kovil temple in Colombo

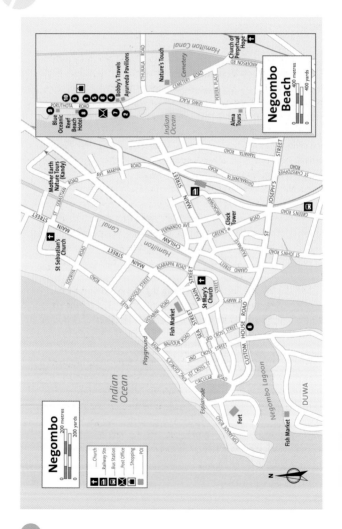

Negombo Beach

- Church of Perpetual Hope
- Hamilton Canal
- Nature's Touch
- Cemetery
- Bobby's Travels
- Ayurveda Pavilions
- Blue Oceanic Beach Hotel
- PORUTHOTA ROAD
- ETHUKALA ROAD
- CEMETERY ROAD
- PEERA PLACE
- LEWIS PLACE
- ANDERSON RD
- Indian Ocean
- Alma Tours
- 0 400 metres
- 0 400 yards

Negombo

- Mother Earth Nature Tours (Kandy)
- St Sebastian's Church
- Hamilton Canal
- Clock Tower
- St Mary's Church
- Fish Market
- Playground
- Fort
- Fish Market
- Negombo Lagoon
- DUWA
- Indian Ocean
- Esplanade

Streets: AVE MARIYA ROAD, TAMMITA ROAD, MAIN STREET, DHARMAWIMALA RAMYA ROAD, ST CHRISTOPHER ROAD, ST JOSEPH'S ROAD, GREEN'S ROAD, BENCHARU RD, FERNANDO AVE, CHILAW STREET, GREEN'S STREET, KURANA, GRAND STREET, ST JOHN'S ROAD, SOORIYA ROAD, COORA ROAD, MAIN STREET, HAMILTON STREET, ASARAPPA ROAD, MAIN STREET, MOSQUE STREET, ALTS STREET, ST MARY'S ROAD, ST MARY'S STREET, CUSTOM HOUSE ROAD, VIDANINI ROAD, BALFOUR ROAD, SEA STREET, DUWA ROAD, 3RD CROSS STREET, 2ND CROSS STREET, KING CROSS STREET, ST CROSS STREET, CIRCULAR ROAD, ESPLANADE ROAD

- Church
- Railway Stn
- Bus Station
- Post Office
- Shopping
- POI

- 0 200 metres
- 0 200 yards

- N

Negombo

Negombo's character is primarily influenced by its proximity to Sri Lanka's international airport. The nearest resort to Bandaranaike (airport), tourists often make the town the first or last stop on their holiday, and as such it has a liveliness lacking in many of the more remote resorts. Most of the action is on the road that runs along the beach, a cluster of lively pubs and restaurants, interspersed with jewellery shops and tour operators. The constant streams of foreign arrivals have pushed the town's development in a Western direction, and walking down the main strip of an evening you'll be met with frequent blasts of 1980s pop and party music emanating from different venues. Many of the places are European owned and run, and this has resulted in a sophisticated entertainment scene, with some upmarket eateries dishing up high-quality European fare. This makes Negombo a good choice for foodies, as well as groups of young – and young-at-heart – tourists after a bit more nightlife than Sri Lanka usually musters.

Besides tourism, fishing also plays a big role in Negombo life, which adds to the place's bustling sense of activity. The distinctive *oruwas*, canoes with large sails, provide an abiding memory – and photo opportunity – and convey the simple, traditional aspects of Sri Lankan coastal life, unchanged by the passage of time and industrialisation. Of course the extent of the local fishing industry means that the town's restaurants never go short of fresh catch, with tuna, shark, herring, mullet, pomfret, crab, lobster and prawns all in plentiful supply. The fishing trade is centred on two fish markets in the town proper, just south of the beach strip. Here you'll also find the town's colonial legacy: churches, Dutch architecture, a fort and a canal, which show that Negombo has more than its convenient location to draw in the crowds.

BEACHES

Negombo has a long, wide beach, some parts of which are in front of the large hotels – and are kept assiduously clean – while other parts are the preserve of the local fisherman, giving the place an authentic, un-touristy feel. Perhaps because they're still recovering from jetlag, many visitors tend to stay around their hotel pools rather than heading down to the sand, so the beach is pleasantly crowd free. There's a football goal for anyone wanting a bit of beach exercise, and the often wide expanse of sand brings out local children for a game of cricket. Plenty of boat trips are also available, as are various watersports.

Swimming is also a possibility, although the resort's exposed position on the coast means the swell can make things risky. There's a flag system in operation to indicate how safe it is to go in the water, and in daylight hours a lifeguard is on duty. While the volume of visitors means that the sands at Negombo are not as pristine as you'll find in the more secluded coastal spots elsewhere, the social side is a good compensation. If you're in town on a Sunday night, head down to the middle section of the beach, where Poruthota and Ethukala roads intersect, where local people gather for a big party, with snack stalls, toys, music and dancing. It's very much a locals' thing rather than something for tourists, but you're likely to receive a warm welcome.

THINGS TO SEE & DO

Ayurveda Pavilions
This stylish, upmarket and expensive Ayurveda centre offers a comprehensive well-being package including curative and preventive treatments for ailments as diverse as gum problems and gynaecological complaints, meditation, yoga and even an Ayurvedic restaurant. Programmes, which run for up to three weeks, are open to both residents and non-residents.

ⓐ Poruthota Road, Ethukala ☏ (031) 227 6719
ⓦ www.ayurvedapavilions.com ⓔ ayurvedapav@eureka.lk

Blue Oceanic

Although not quite as posh as the Ayurveda Pavilions, the centre at the Blue Oceanic has cheaper treatments on offer, including massage, some of which are for extended periods.

ⓐ Poruthota Road ❶ (031) 227 9000 ⓔ blueoceanic@sltnet.lk

Bobby's Travels

Small, informal office from where you can rent a car, bike or motorbike, and book fishing or lagoon trips. English, German and French are spoken. There are no fixed prices, so use your negotiating skills.

ⓐ 20D Poruthota Road ❶ (031) 227 4549 or 077 304 2695
ⓦ www.bobbytravelslk.com ⓔ info@bobbytravelslk.com
🕑 09.00–22.00 ❶ Cash only

Mother Earth Nature Tours

Highly recommended operator, offering hiking, canoeing, rafting, cycling, birdwatching, horse riding, safaris, camping and tailor-made tours.

🔺 *Negombo is a fishing village*

ⓐ Office based in Kandy ⓣ 777 840 001 ⓕ (081) 247 0156
ⓦ www.earth-srilanka.com ⓔ ndsilva67@yahoo.com

New Reef Beach Hotel
The hotel runs PADI scuba-diving courses both for beginners and
advanced divers, plus snorkelling at 09.00 daily.
ⓐ 47 Poruthota Road ⓣ (031) 531 2121 ⓦ www.rani-holiday-village.com

TAKING A BREAK

Outside Colombo and other larger towns, the distinction between
restaurants, cafés and bars seldom applies. In the resort, there's little
financial incentive to restrict your business to just drinks or snacks:
the vast majority of places open early, usually between 07.00 and
08.00, serve breakfast, and a range of snacks, light bites, main meals
and drinks all day, before closing between 22.00 and 24.00, depending
on how busy the resort is. Most places are highly customer-orientated,
and if a group of you wants to stay later, entrepreneurial Sri Lankans
are likely to accommodate you. In the listings, cafés, restaurants and
bars are listed separately where appropriate, but otherwise most
places will be geared up to serve you what you're after, whether light,
heavy or liquid.

AFTER DARK

Restaurants
Honky Tonky Two £ ❶ Friendly place with elephant murals on the
wall and bargain food that comes recommended. ⓐ 46 Poruthota Road
ⓣ (031) 531 0800 ⓛ 09.00–23.00 ❶ Accepts payment in foreign currency

Players £ ❷ Cheap-and-cheerful pub and restaurant in a big house.
Nightly karaoke and a pool table upstairs pull in the punters.
ⓐ 20 Poruthota Road ⓣ (031) 227 8977 or 077 707 6485
ⓔ players_pool@yahoo.com ⓛ 10.00–01.00 ❶ Cash only

○ *Fresh produce is used in Sri Lankan cooking*

Sherry Land £ ❸ Amiable and low-key pub and restaurant that has some very pleasant outside tables and an air-conditioned interior. It's done out a bit like a log cabin, and there's a good selection of imported and local wine and spirits plus cocktails. The seafood comes recommended. ⓐ 74 Poruthota Road ❶ (031) 487 3125 ❻ 11.00–23.00 ❶ Accepts credit cards

Alta Italia ££ ❹ If you fancy a change from rice and curry, try this Italian-run restaurant, which imports its ingredients from home and turns them into authentic Italian favourites, such as pizza, risotto, lasagne and a gamut of other pasta dishes. There's also proper Italian coffee and tiramisu. The place is decorated in typically Latin style, with large, plush, red armchairs, bench-style outside tables and a Ferrari flag. ⓐ 36 Poruthota Road ❶ (031) 227 9206 ❻ 08.00–24.00

Bijou ££ ❺ Swiss-owned restaurant that pins its patriotic colours to the wall in the form of Swiss flags. It's very big and very busy, serving up Chinese, Italian, seafood and – as you might have guessed – fondue. Particularly popular with German-speaking tourists. Food and atmosphere are both great. ⓐ 44 Poruthota Road ❶ (031) 531 9577 ❻ 09.00–22.30 ❶ Accepts credit cards

Choy's Restaurant ££ ❻ This large air-conditioned restaurant overlooks the fishing harbour and is popular with tourists and locals who want to get away from the bustle of Poruthota Road. Mainly Chinese dishes are served here, but also on offer are Indian curries and pizzas. Finish off with fresh fruit salad or go for a caramel pudding. There's a pastry shop at street level and a takeaway service too. ⓐ 31 Custom House Road ❶ 943 122 22807 or 943 1223 8345 ❻ 09.00–23.00

King Coconut ££ ❼ Big and basic restaurant that's popular with locals as well as tourists. A sign there prohibits hard liquor, but this is more than compensated for by the romantic tables on the beach. Great value

food from East and West, with the curries particularly acclaimed.
ⓐ 11 Poruthota Road ⓣ (031) 227 8043 ⓛ 09.00–23.00 or 24.00
ⓘ Accepts credit cards

Rodeo ££ ❽ Something of a Negombo legend, you can find Rodeo by listening out for the loud 1980s party hits that it pumps out into the street. Always packed and popular, this no-frills pub and restaurant seats happy holidaymakers at plain tables and benches, but nobody seems to mind. The animal skull on the wall wearing a Santa hat sums up the irreverent party vibe. ⓐ 35A Poruthota Road ⓣ (031) 222 1345 or (094) 777 746 474 ⓔ janakad@yahoo.co.uk ⓛ 09.00–24.00

Blue Oceanic £££ ❾ One of the more atmospheric hotel-restaurants, with nicely spaced-out tables that extend on to the beach, plus some sofas for extra comfortable dining. As well as a buffet, they have a decent range of vegetarian and Italian dishes, and a mellow live band that goes from table to table. ⓐ Poruthota Road ⓣ (031) 227 9000-3 ⓔ blueoceanic@sltnet.lk ⓛ 06.30–10.00, 12.30–15.00, 19.30–22.00 ⓘ Accepts credit cards

Lords £££ ❿ Classy, stylish and modern fairy-lit restaurant whose cricket theme should not suggest a tacky 'Brits abroad' type of place, because this is far from that. An excellent range of food from all over the world including some choice Thai mains and rare specials like New Zealand lamb that you can enjoy on leather seats overlooking a Japanese-style pond with catfish – who are not on the menu. There's also an adjoining bar and nightclub. ⓐ 80B Poruthota Road ⓣ (031) 227 5566 ⓛ 18.00–22.00 Tues–Sun, closed Mon ⓘ Accepts credit cards

Tangalla

One of the furthest main resorts from the capital, Tangalla, also known as Tangalle, is a simple town, 35 km (22 miles) east of Matara and free from the large-scale development seen in some tourist towns further west. It has a laid-back atmosphere, ideal for a lazy holiday. Bisecting the village itself is a freshwater lagoon and river, the mouth of which sees much of Tangalla's fishing activity. While its stretch of sand is pretty enough to merit a visit, the place is more than just a beach town; it has a handful of other attractions in its favour. The nearby blowhole is an established stop on the tourist trail and makes a great nature spot, and an impressive rock temple and the huge Buddha at Wewurukannala, both within easy reach, show a religious aspect to the area.

BEACHES

Tourists have found their way back to Tangalla following the tsunami, but it remains a tranquil place and visitors will be able to find a quiet spot on the beach. If you don't end up alone, it's just as likely that any other footsteps will be canine as human: friendly dogs seem to enjoy relaxing on the narrow stretch of sand. The shoreline is rocky, giving Tangalla a more rugged look than other resorts. Coconut palms overhang the quiet beach and provide shade for a sloping grassy knoll that separates the sand and road, a popular meeting point for locals. Nature lovers will enjoy the beach's abundant lining of purple flowers, and the smattering of boats bear testament to the village's fishing traditions. While swimming is usually safe, in summer the currents can become forceful, and weaker swimmers should take particular care. Tangalla residents unperturbed by this are the dolphins; occasionally they venture close to the coast and can be spotted by observant sunbathers. Because the coast in this area is east facing, Tangalla is a good place to watch the sunrise.

Tangalla's shoreline can be divided into several distinct areas. To the north is a long stretch of white sand called Medaketiya beach, which enjoys some of the safest swimming conditions; much of the accommodation is based here. West of the main town you find the posher Pallikaduwa and its pretty rock recesses. Both here and in Goyambokka, even further west, the natural divisions allow some of the guesthouses to offer their guests access to a private beach.

◆ *Fishermen at Tangalla beach*

🔺 *Tangalla beach's palm trees line the shore*

TAKING A BREAK

Bars & cafés

Sana's Bar £ From the beach, climb the steps, which are made of tyres, to reach this thatched place. Sample some tea, lime juice, soft drinks and fried rice at one of the four tables. ⓐ On the beach ⓣ No phone ⓛ Irregular hours

AFTER DARK

Restaurants

Eva Lanka ££ Italian food dominates this air-conditioned pizzeria at Eva Lanka Hotel, with a few Sri Lankan standard dishes thrown in for good measure. An open-air bar serves drinks and snacks. ⓐ On the beach ⓣ (047) 224 0940 ⓦ www.eva.lk ⓔ hoteleva@sltnet.lk

Amanwella £££ Top-quality hotel restaurant with glass walls and swimming pool. The chef uses ingredients from the hotel gardens to craft a variety of unusual and impressive dishes. ⓐ Bodhi Mw, Wella Mawatha, Godellawela ⓣ (047) 224 1333 ⓦ www.amanwella.com

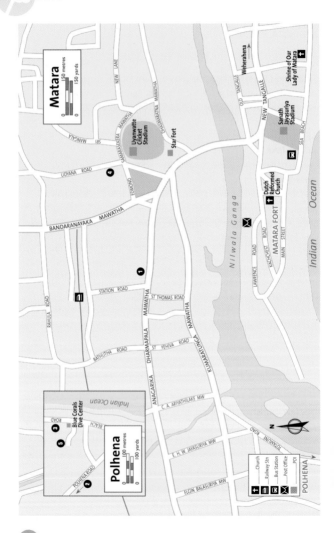

Matara

As much a bustling town as a beach resort, Matara (pronounced without the middle 'a') offers a generous helping of activities, sights and entertainment, as well as a large, fine beach. It will suit anyone who wants more from their holiday than just lying on the beach, and its two complementary cricket grounds are particular draws for tourists who want to experience one of the islanders' top passions first hand. Cow-drawn rickshaws wend their way among the motorised traffic, an eye-catching image of the juxtapositions of modern Sri Lanka. A nearby university gives Matara a youthful, vibrant feel, and the thriving local industry adds to its liveliness, which can make a welcome change if you're arriving from one of the island's smaller, sleepier beach towns. If, however, you do yearn for some seclusion and tranquillity, try the small suburb of Polhena, whose budget accommodation and quiet beach draw in some tourists, particularly over the weekend, although it never feels crowded.

Matara has a European feel. Much of the Dutch-era architecture is still in evidence, and the city fort still exerts a colonial presence. A mosque and temple join the couple of churches in illustrating the town's various influences. The town sits among lush paddy fields, spice plantations and tea estates.

BEACHES

With fine, white sand, Matara's gently sloping wide stretch of coastline sees few tourists, perhaps because the town is not primarily thought of as a beach resort. There are few beach shacks, and the landscaping and restoration work needed following the tsunami is now complete.

Polhena is the more popular beach option in the area. Wide, private and surrounded wherever you look by leaning coconut trees, it's a delightfully relaxing place, and is enjoyed by the Sri Lankans, whose children can sometimes be seen in the morning taking swimming lessons. The clear, calm water facilitates not only swimming but snorkelling too, and unlike in some resorts this can sometimes be possible even during the monsoon season. Boat trips and diving are other options.

THINGS TO SEE & DO

Blue Corals Dive Center

Blue Coral will rent licensed diver's equipment, and also offers snorkelling and river tours to see crocodiles, birds, buffalo and paddy fields.

ⓐ 36 Beach Road, Polhena ⓣ 077 716 3685 or 077 760 0803
ⓔ bluecoralspolhena@yahoo.com

🔺 *Cricket is the most popular sport in Sri Lanka*

Cricket

Matara has two cricket grounds. The main Uyanwatte Stadium is used for local matches, but first class and international matches are not played here. The Sanath Jayasuriya Stadium, named after the so-called 'Master Blaster of Matara', stages softball cricket, but the games here often bear more resemblance to carnivals than sporting contests, with live music, refreshments and circus-style performers.

Uyanwatte ⓐ Edmond Samarasekera Mw, by Star Fort
Sanath Jayasuriya ⓐ Sea Beach Road, by bus station

Shrine of Our Lady of Matara

Set in some neat and pleasant gardens, the church is open for services on Tuesday at 17.00, Wednesday, Thursday and Friday at 06.45, Saturday at 07.00 and Sunday at 08.00.

ⓐ Matara Beach Road ⓣ (041) 222 2056 ⓦ www.stmarychmatara.org

Weherahena

The village temple boasts a 39-m (128-ft) high Buddha statue, part of a large temple complex including statues of snakes and lions, candle-lit shrines, a photo and portrait gallery and a man-made cave with 200 comic-book-style scenes on the walls. The part of the compound that houses the monks is off limits to the public. There's a smattering of shops at the entrance, selling religious souvenirs, camera film, drinks and ice creams, with a few tables to sit at, plus a batik shop and training centre.

ⓐ A few kilometres east of Matara ⓒ Around 06.30–18.00
ⓝ Bus: 9, 34 from Matara

TAKING A BREAK

Bars & cafés

Galle Oriental Bakery £ ❶ It's not at all touristy or up to date, but the friendly and helpful staff at the small Galle Oriental Bakery do their best to make you enjoy your visit, and the fans, too, are most welcome. On the menu you'll find fruit, pastry, fish, eggs, roti, sausages, biscuits, ice cream, sweets and cakes. ⓐ Anagarika Dharmapala Mw ❶ (041) 222 6582 🕐 07.00–19.30

A Taste of Sri Lanka ££ ❷ An initiative of Sarvodaya, Sri Lanka's biggest charity, this community centre and restaurant is run by local women and was designed to allow visitors to mix with the village community while sampling some traditional entertainment. There are cooking demonstrations on Saturdays from 11.00–12.00, and for groups who call ahead. The abstemious will like it particularly, because there's no smoking, no alcohol and no meat. ⓐ Polhena Road ❶ (608) 442 5945 ⓦ www.sarvodaya.org 🕐 09.00–17.00

AFTER DARK

Restaurants
Orchid Restaurant £ ❸ Renowned for seafood and fish, this restaurant also includes Asian and European food on the menu. Crocodile safari trips can also be organised along the Niwala River. ⓐ Polhena Reef Gardens Hotel, 30 Beach Road, Polhena ❶ (041) 222 2478 ⓦ www.prghotel.com ⓔ info@prghotel.com 🕐 08.00–23.00

Samanmal £ ❹ Predominantly a Chinese restaurant, Samanmal also has some Western, particularly Italian options. It's a large restaurant and on the second floor of the building that houses it. ⓐ 64 Udyana Road ❶ (041) 222 4828 ❶ (041) 222 6058 🕐 08.30–22.30 ❶ Cash only

Sunil's Rest ££ ❺ This popular restaurant serves Eastern, Western and Sri Lankan cuisine. Sunil's has some picnic tables in an agreeable garden area. They also rent bikes and motorbikes. ⓐ Second crossroads, Polhena beach ❶ (041) 222 1983 🕐 24 hours

Mirissa

Coastal resorts don't come much more perfect-looking than Mirissa, at the east end of Weligama bay. Its guesthouses are less strung out than in its neighbouring resort, which gives it a little more atmosphere, although it's still a sleepy spot that will please holidaymakers for whom the beauty of nature is the number one priority. The town itself, whose name means 'shell village', developed on the back of the fishing industry and retains the charming ambience of such a place today.

BEACHES

A beautiful, idyllic beach ringed by coconut palms and greenery, Mirissa's position, tucked inside an inlet, gives it a sense of privacy and seclusion, as do the trees that line the back of the sand, almost making you forget about the world behind. The beach is flat with a few sunbeds, and some of the local businesses have put out tables and chairs so you can enjoy your meal or drinks on the sand. The sea is such a spot-on shade of blue that it looks as though it has been digitally enhanced, but while it may look inviting, the safety for swimming varies from place to place along the shore, so it's a good idea to make enquiries before taking the plunge. For the energetic, there's also a volleyball net and a choice of watersports, although thankfully for the resort's tranquillity, not the petrol-powered, noisy ones. The clear water offers good snorkelling opportunities, and you can also go fishing, whale-watching, kayaking or on a boat trip.

THINGS TO SEE & DO

Secret Root Ayurveda

This small and simple spa comes recommended for both service and atmosphere. Options include Ayurvedic oil massage, herbal punch

◆ The palm-fringed beach at Mirissa

massage, shirodara head treatment and herbal steam baths.
An Ayurvedic doctor can also be called upon for consultation.
ⓐ 300 m (385 ft) off main road, by temple ☎ 077 329 4332

Wadiya

As well as Ayurveda treatments, Wadiya will rent you motorbikes,
bodyboards and surfboards, or take you snorkelling or on a boat tour.
☎ (041) 225 1574 or 077 950 6074 🕒 07.30–last customer

TAKING A BREAK

Bars & cafés

Dealing £ Seafood is the main idea at this wooden-themed place, which hosts
DJ parties at night. ⓐ On the beach ☎ No phone 🕒 06.00–last customer

Wadiya ££ Wadiya pins its laid-back colours to the wall with a
Bob Marley poster up against the wooden interior. There's plenty of
fish, as you'd expect, and a good range of juices and sandwiches.
ⓐ On the beach ☎ (041) 225 1574, 077 950 6074 🕒 07.30–last customer

AYURVEDA

Ayurvedic medicine originated in India several thousand years
ago. Its name comes from the Sanskrit *ayur* (life) and *veda*
(science or knowledge). Now used in the Western world as a
complementary or alternative medicine, the aim of Ayurveda is to
balance the body, mind and spirit, thereby bringing health and
happiness. It is believed to prevent illness and promote wellness.
Ayurveda therapies involve various treatments to cleanse the body
and restore balance, for example the use of herbs, massage, yoga
and meditation. If taken seriously, Ayurveda treatment will involve
changes in diet, lifestyle and habits. There are many specialist
centres and hotels offering Ayurvedic programmes in Sri Lanka.

AFTER DARK

Restaurants

Sunset £ Amiable and great-value fish restaurant with a thatched roof, pine tables and a tiled floor. It's friendly and quiet, and you can take your meals on to the beach. There's also a book swap. Look out for the daily specials. ⓐ Bandara Mulla, on the beach ① 077 734 0434 ⓛ 06.00–01.00 or 02.00

Café Mirissa ££ Loud reggae music emanates from Café Mirissa, whose bare, stone floor keeps it pleasantly cool. The fish is brought in fresh from the market every day, and there are occasional barbecues. ⓐ On the beach ① 077 747 7203 ⓛ Approx. 08.00–last customer

Weligama

The name Weligama means 'sandy village', and this is one instance where the connection between name and place is overwhelmingly obvious. Despite the beauty of the wide, long, crescent-shaped beach, mass tourism has not yet permeated the town, and it remains a quiet spot for Sri Lanka connoisseurs to relax away from the crowds. Shopping opportunities are mostly limited to the few handicraft shops. There's little in the way of nightlife or entertainment, so travellers who end up here are usually solely after some R&R. That or perhaps watersports: decent waves make Weligama a stop on the surf trail, and there are also scuba-diving possibilities.

BEACHES

Fishing is still an important part of Weligama life, and a visit here offers you the chance to see stilt fishermen, who use skills to snare their catch that tourists may be more likely to see on display at the circus. This is one of the few remaining places where such people are likely to be the genuine article – elsewhere posing on the stilts for photos has proved more lucrative to local entrepreneurs than bothering to catch fish.

Weligama is not quite as immaculate as the beach at nearby Mirissa – the main road is closer to the sand than is ideal, and at some points the sea is too murky to swim in (your guesthouse staff should be able to advise you on where to go for a dip). But the shoreline is still a stunning sight, and distinguishes itself with Taprobane, a tiny island just a couple of hundred metres out to sea, which hosts a gorgeous villa. Built by an eccentric count in the 1920s, today the exclusive five-bedroom luxury property can be rented by anyone who has the cash and doesn't mind wading through the water to reach it. The beach is also the venue of the Ceylon Elephant Polo Association Championships, held in February each year, which make fascinating entertainment.

THINGS TO SEE & DO

Bavarian Divers

This is a German-run operation offering the usual full range of diving courses, as well as underwater photography, snorkelling, boat rides and other watersports.

ⓐ 142 Sri Sangagada Mw, Kapparatota ❶ (091) 415 0201 or (077) 785 8330 (mobile) Ⓦ www.cbg.de/bavariandivers ⓔ bbasdive@sltnet.lk

TAKING A BREAK

As is common in the smaller resorts, you won't find separate cafés as such, but the restaurants listed all serve breakfast, lunch and snacks throughout the day.

AFTER DARK

Restaurants

Weligama is not known for its restaurant scene, and the majority of tourists end up eating at their guesthouses.

Thisara £ With a wooden interior and pine furniture, Thisara's extensive menu includes various snacks and light meals plus pizza, Italian and Sri Lankan food including a selection of devilled dishes and curries.
ⓐ 21 New Galle Road, opposite side to beach ❶ 077 329 4927
🕙 10.00–22.00

Crystal Villa ££ Seafood is the speciality of this nicely appointed hotel restaurant, which serves both Western and Eastern cuisine.
ⓐ Galle–Matara Road, Palena ❶ (041) 225 0635 🕙 24 hours

Unawatuna

Rich in mythology, biodiversity and character, Unawatuna is a firm favourite among the backpacker crowd. Despite its obvious charms – gently sloping white sands encircled by palms, a protected bay area keeping swimmers safe all year long, and a lively nightlife (by Sri Lankan standards, of course) – it has not suffered the excessive commercialisation undergone by some resorts, and as a result feels less polished and more authentic, which is probably why it pulls in so many independent travellers. The name Unawatuna means 'there it fell', and the resort's attractions do seem haphazardly thrown together, with casual eateries and little souvenir shops dotted around.

BEACHES

Unawatuna's beach is variously trumpeted as the best one in south or west Sri Lanka, depending on where the enthusiast decides it is. Fringed with palm trees, the bay curves round beautifully, and the narrow beach slopes down to the sea. Assortments of rocks separate the sand into rugged, picturesque sections, while the reef prevents larger waves from reaching the shore, a boon for swimmers. The beach draws in both foreigners – usually young backpackers, and local sunseekers – and the mixed crowd creates a fun, happening vibe that distinguishes Unawatuna from the quieter, pristine sands peopled by just a handful of tourists. However, while this is one of the island's more crowded tourist beaches, the number of visitors never becomes oppressive, and there's still plenty of space and sunbeds.

Beach industry is thriving in Unawatuna. The sand is peppered with herbal massage outfits, and there are also plenty of places where you can pick up an inflatable dinghy or – if you'd prefer a sturdier vessel – book a trip in a glass-bottomed boat. Other shoreline distractions include surfing lessons, while native visitors often start up a game of sea volleyball. The less energetically-inclined can just doze in a hammock.

THINGS TO SEE & DO

Hotel Flower Garden

Detox-based and general Ayurvedic programmes are offered,
including oil-anointing therapy, herbal baths and massage, as well
as tailored health treatments. Programmes generally run from three
to fourteen days.

ⓐ Wella Dewala Road ☎ (091) 222 5286
ⓦ www.hotelflowergarden.com ⓔ flowerga@gmail.com
🕐 09.00–17.00 ❶ Credit cards accepted

🔺 A herbal massage or some Ayurveda is easy to come across in Unawatuna

Secret Garden

A yoga teacher runs public lessons during the holiday season, starting at 08.00. It's also possible to book the entire facility, which includes a dedicated yoga dome, and learn as a group of up to 12–14 people. Ayurveda, massage, acupuncture and meditation are also available.

ⓐ Just off the beach ① 077 761 4119 or (091) 224 1857
ⓦ www.secretgardenvilla.lk ⓔ secretgardenvilla@yahoo.com

Sonja's Garden

As well as serving a range of healthfood, including muesli, salad and burritos, which you can munch on in her greenhouses, Sonja runs cookery lessons starting at 11.00, so you can perfect your Sri Lankan rice and curry. Many of the ingredients are fresh from the garden itself.

ⓐ 52 Yadehimulla Road ① (091) 224 5815 or 077 961 5310 ① Early–19.00

Submarine Diving School

With 30 years' experience, the Submarine Diving School runs PADI courses, jungle beach tours and snorkelling outings.

ⓐ On beach, Wella Dewala Road ① 777 196 753
ⓦ www.divinginsrilanka.com ⓔ shirly_diving@hotmail.com
① 09.00–18.00 ① Cash only

Unawatuna Diving Centre

PADI scuba-diving courses for advanced divers (including rescue) and beginners from German- and English-speaking instructors. Night and wreck diving and snorkelling and equipment hire are other options. For the best conditions, the recommended time for diving in Sri Lanka is mid-October to the end of April. During the rest of the year the sea can be too rough and visibility is poorer.

ⓐ Matara Beach Road ① (091) 224 4693 or 077 790 3430
ⓦ www.unawatunadiving.com ⓔ info@unawatunadiving.com
① 08.30–18.00, mid-Oct–end Apr

TAKING A BREAK

Bars & cafés

Imesh £ This bright, friendly and cheerful all-day café serves a range of snacks, light meals and seafood. **ⓐ** On the beach **ⓣ** No phone **ⓛ** 07.00–last customer

Surfer's Break £ Famed chocolate brownies are the highlight of this laid-back café-come-surf shop, where the predominantly English and Italian food is eaten on low seats and cushions. If you're anxious to get back to the waves, they also do takeaway sandwiches. **ⓐ** On the beach **ⓣ** No phone **ⓛ** 08.00–11.00, 19.00–24.00

Zimmer £ An Unawatuna long-timer, this vegetarian eatery rustles up organic food from an impressive variety of cuisines including Indonesian, Indian, Chinese, Greek, Mexican, Thai, Lebanese, Italian, Japanese and Sri Lankan, plus some tempting avocado dishes, all prepared by a British chef. A book exchange and pleasant, shady verandah give it a nice atmosphere, and free meditation instruction and massages are also offered. **ⓐ** Wella Dewala Road, by bus stop **ⓣ** (091) 438 0366 or 077 628 5192 **ⓔ** jinsen_2004@hotmail.com

Dilena Beach Resort ££ Simple seafront eatery serving seafood, beef, prawns and devilled dishes, plus a range of sandwiches. **ⓐ** Matara Road, on seafront opposite little beach south of main stretch **ⓣ** (091) 228 3230 **ⓛ** 07.00–22.00

AFTER DARK

Restaurants

Coral Light £ There are plenty of drinks on the menu for thirsty surfers and sunbathers as well as fresh seafood, Chinese, Italian and pizza at this cheap and cheerful place. **ⓐ** On the beach **ⓣ** 077 965 6144 **ⓛ** 08.00–last customer, usually 01.00 or 02.00

Hard Rock ££ Hard Rock's tables on the sand are one element that brings the tourists to this beach shack, the extensive cocktail list is another enticement. ⓐ On the beach ⓣ (091) 224 6288 or 077 795 1969 ⓛ 07.30–00.30

Hotel Flower Garden ££ A step up from the usual resort eatery, the bright and clean restaurant at Hotel Flower Garden adds a touch of class with glass-topped tables and wicker chairs. Plants and displays show the management's attention to detail, and you'll be kept cool with fans. The food is European and Sri Lankan. ⓐ Wella Dewala Road ⓣ (091) 222 5286 ⓦ www.hotelflowergarden.com ⓔ flowerga@gmail.com ⓛ 08.00–23.00

● A range of watersports is available at Unawatuna beach

Pink Elephant ££ Large eatery with outside tables, and solid wooden chairs and tables – a refreshing change from the usual cheap plastic. Enjoy a piece of freshly-made cake with an Italian coffee. On Friday nights the Pink Elephant holds a Sri Lankan curry buffet from 19.30. ⓐ Centre of the beach ⓣ 077 358 5034 ⓔ podisignor@yahoo.de ⓛ 08.00–23.30

Rock View ££ Funky orange beach shack serving up fresh seafood and Chinese mains. ⓐ On the beach ⓣ 077 706 9454 ⓛ 09.00–last customer

Sea View ££ Simple beachside family-run restaurant dishing up everything from hearty breakfasts, informal lunches to evening meals. Try spicy or non-spicy curries, freshly caught seafood or go for straightforward pastas and pizzas. ⓐ Dewala Road ⓣ (091) 222 4376 ⓦ www.seaviewunawatuna.com ⓔ seaview@sltnet.lk ⓛ 07.00–23.00

Thaproban ££ Refurbished in 2008, this beachside restaurant with its luxury décor creates mellow vibes and is renowned for the food, which is prepared using ayurvedic principles. The menu includes Sri Lankan and international fare and a good wine list. The sister place, Thambapanni Retreat, on Yaddehimulla Road, also offers seafood dishes in a stylish ambience and closes when the last customer leaves. ⓐ On the beach ⓣ (091) 438 1722 or 077 790 1599 ⓦ www.thambapannileisure.com ⓔ info@thambapannileisure.com ⓛ 07.00–23.00 or last customer ❶ Credit cards accepted

Thilak ££ Breakfast, sandwiches, pancakes, omelettes, plus Chinese and Italian main meals including pizza, in a cool, airy interior. ⓐ Dewala Road ⓣ (091) 438 0356 or 077 717 7604 ⓛ 07.30–22.00 or 23.00

Upul ££ Located in the middle of Unawatuna's main beach, Upul provides you with a cool oasis from the sun. With its wooden, fan-equipped interior, Upul's menu features predominantly Sri Lankan and Italian food plus Italian wine. ⓐ On the beach ⓣ (091) 438 4387 or 077 606 7170 ⓔ ajith999@hotmail.com ⓛ 07.30–23.00

⬢ *Unawatuna beach with a famous* Dagoba *in the background*

The Villa ££ Plenty of salads, including Russian and Greek, are on the menu at this friendly and professional hotel restaurant, whose clean white tiles and fans give it a bright and airy feel. The garden has sturdy wooden tables, and there's a pleasant sea view. ⓐ On the beach ⓣ (091) 224 7253

Comoran Beach Club £££ Almost like a temple in design, this large, stylish and atmospheric venue is one of the coolest places on the beach to eat. Clean and modern, the attention that has gone into every aspect of the décor and menu is evident. ⓐ Yaddehimulla Road ⓣ (091) 438 1337 ⓦ diyakawa@sltnet.lk ⓛ 07.30–last customer

Full Moon £££ Italian-run beachfront restaurant with a decent range of pastas and Italian coffee. There are some Chinese options and some quality seafood, including prawns and lobster. The kitchen closes at 22.00. ⓐ Yaddehimulla Road ⓣ (091) 438 1337 ⓕ (091) 438 1337 ⓦ www.fullmoonvillage.com ⓛ 07.00–23.00 or 24.00

Galle

In the south of Sri Lanka, the town of Galle showcases colonial Sri Lanka at its most delightful, combining Dutch architecture and atmosphere with a bustling, typically Sri Lankan centre, all topped off with some of the finest dining outside Colombo. What Galle lacks in miles of pristine coastline, it more than makes up for in heritage and culture. The modern city is lively and industrial, with horns blaring in narrow streets, music emanating from small shops and public speaker systems blaring out news of various civic gatherings. Local traders here are particularly keen to persuade you to peruse their wares, and there are some colourful fruit stalls and souvenir shops, where you can pick up bright and kitschy religious souvenirs.

Going south, the other side of Galle cricket ground, the atmosphere changes totally. The well-preserved Dutch quarter, or Fort, has retained a laid-back, colonial appeal and its charms won international recognition 20 years ago when it was awarded the status of a UNESCO World

⬤ *A bird's eye view of Galle Fort*

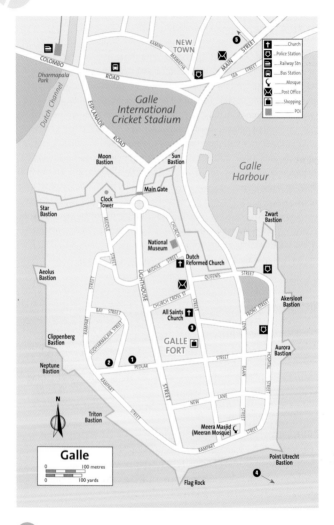

Galle

0 — 100 metres
0 — 100 yards

	Church
	Police Station
	Railway Stn
	Bus Station
	Mosque
	Post Office
	Shopping
	POI

Heritage Site. Indeed, the fortifications proved they were still fit for purpose during the 2004 tsunami, sparing the old quarter much of the damage inflicted on the modern centre. Here you'll also find narrow streets, but far from being filled with blaring tuk-tuks (cabin cycles), they are near silent, and it's pleasant to have a slow wander around the area, taking in the colourful colonial façades and upmarket jewellery boutiques. The quarter is also something of an Islamic enclave, with a mosque and Arabic college.

BEACHES

Visitors are more likely to come to Galle for its heritage than its beach. Much of the rugged coastline is rocky, rather than sandy. That said, there are gentler beach parts, and the sands here suffer in comparison with the island's high average – elsewhere, they would seem great. Fishing still plays a role in Galle life, which is evident in the fish stalls that line the coast and the trawlers on the beach. For security reasons, photography is prohibited in some areas on the coast.

THINGS TO SEE & DO

Dutch Reformed Church
One of the city's finest buildings from the colonial era, the church is worth a look for both its beautiful white exterior and its interior, where the most memorable feature is the often touching memorials to some of the Dutch inhabitants of the time.
ⓐ Corner of Middle Street and Church Street ● 08.00–16.30

Dutch villas
One of the most picturesque legacies of colonialism, the many Dutch-era villas scattered around Galle bring unexpected dashes of colour and charm to the Sri Lankan coast, and recall a Europe long lost to modern development in many other places.
ⓐ Around town

◔ *Remnants of the Dutch colonial era: Galle's Dutch Reformed Church*

Galle Fort

The Fort is an area of town, rather than a specific site in itself. A World Heritage Site, it is the largest remaining fortress in Asia, built by invaders from Europe. Many of its ramparts remain in excellent condition, giving the town a rugged, windswept European feel quite different from that of Sri Lanka's beach resorts. Because of the high number of tourists who visit the fort, some of the more popular parts have seen small market stalls spring up, and visitors are also liable to be approached by hawkers. The tourist presence has also encouraged another group: young men who are willing to jump the 15 metres (48 ft) from the ramparts into the sea below for a small sum.

ⓐ South of International Cricket Stadium

Meera Masjid (Meeran Mosque)

Overlooking the sea, the century-old mosque is best viewed on Friday at prayer time. Five times a day the Muezzin's call to prayer rings out from the minaret outside. Some areas are segregated by gender.

ⓐ Corner of Leyn Baan Street and Rampart Street

TAKING A BREAK

Bars & cafés

Pedlar's Inn Café ££ ❶ Small eatery housed in a yellow Dutch villa, with a few pleasant tables on a terrace looking out onto the street. The menu includes light snacks such as sandwiches, toasties and milkshakes.

ⓐ 92 Pedlar Street ❶ No phone ❶ 10.00–18.00

AFTER DARK

Restaurants

Thanks to the gentrification of the Fort area, many of Galle's dining options are stylish upmarket eateries. The quality of the food and establishment is typically high – as are the prices – relative to most Sri Lankan resorts.

Mrs Khalid's Guesthouse ££ ❷ Highly-regarded guesthouse restaurant, whose owner is renowned for being able to prepare any dish upon request. Alcohol isn't permitted. ⓐ 102 Pedlar Street ❶ (091) 223 4907 ● 08.00–22.00 ❶ Book ahead

Galle Fort Hotel £££ ❸ Run by Australian expats, this marvellously classy hotel-restaurant is separated from the street by Mediterranean-style shutters. Inside, the high ceilings, superb food and chic atmosphere attract lots of foreigners. Offers modern Asian cuisine. ⓐ 28 Church Street, Galle Fort ❶ (091) 223 2870 or 077 790 6028 ⓔ karlsteinberg@galleforthotel.com ● 11.30–23.30

Pepper £££ ❹ Top-quality hotel-restaurant set on a beautiful beachfront, its trendy interior has a hint of Japanese minimalism. The food is a modern fusion of international and Sri Lankan. There is also a good wine list. ⓐ The Fortress, Koggala Beach ❶ (091) 438 0909 ❶ (091) 438 0338 Ⓦ www.thefortress.lk ● 07.00–23.00

The Sun House £££ ❺ High-class, atmospheric restaurant with a candlelit verandah and garden, ideal for a romantic dinner for two. Seafood features significantly on the menu, which betrays influences from Thailand, Sri Lanka, Australia and the Mediterranean in weird and wonderful combinations. ⓐ 18 Upper Dickson Road ❶ (091) 438 0275 Ⓦ www.thesunhouse.com ● 07.30–23.00

Hikkaduwa

One of the first beaches to start attracting foreign crowds, Hikkaduwa was once a hippie hotspot, and has retained its alternative vibe by continuing to pull in backpackers and budget travellers, plus the surfers drawn by the big waves. The young, excitable crowd gives the town an energetic feel that's relatively rare in sleepy Sri Lanka, and Hikkaduwa can often feel more like Goa, with occasional concerts on the beach. It's not the most pristine resort, but its relaxed mood and cheap accommodation suit those out to enjoy some nights out and days doing watersports without spending too much.

BEACHES

While Hikkaduwa's large waves are fantastic for the surfing crowd, they do mean that swimming can be risky, and only strong swimmers should think about going for a bathe. Going in for watersports is another matter, and there are plenty of options here: the resort has the island's highest concentration of diving schools, which also offer wreck and reef dives thanks to the proximity of both. Divers should head to the southern part of the coastline, Wewala.

Although it's fair to say that Hikkaduwa is not quite as picture perfect as some of the less developed resorts, in most other countries not blessed with Sri Lanka's wealth of stunning sands, it would be considered an excellent beach. Enjoy watching the sunset against the pretty fishing boats bobbing on the sea. You might also spot a turtle, some of which venture quite close to the shore.

THINGS TO SEE & DO

Barracuda Diving Centre

Barracuda's experienced divers offer PADI courses plus other watersports.
ⓐ 356c Galle Road ⓣ (091) 492 5154 or 077 747 9824
ⓦ www.hikkaduwabarracuda.com ⓔ diving_wasantha@yahoo.com

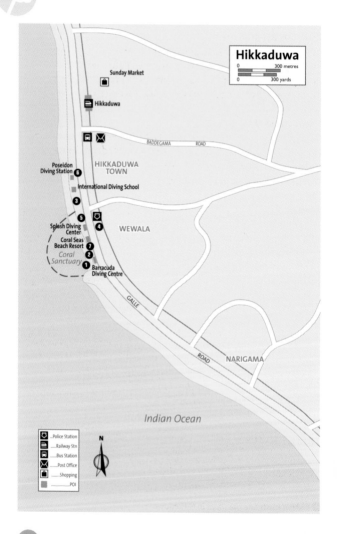

Coral Seas Beach Resort

As well as offering diving, deep-sea fishing and snorkelling, this hotel-based operator runs tours and trips on a glass-bottomed boat.

ⓐ 346 Galle Road ⓣ (091) 227 7248 or 077 790 8516

ⓦ www.coralseashikkaduwa.com ⓔ coralseas@sltnet.lk

International Diving School

Friendly, family-run outfit staffed by PADI, CMAS and UDI trained divers.

ⓐ Coral Sands Hotel, 326 Galle Road ⓣ 072 223 1683 ⓕ (091) 227 6541

ⓦ www.internationaldivingschool.com

ⓔ internationaldivingschool@hotmail.com

⬤ *Fishing boats line the shore in Hikkaduwa*

Poseidon Diving Station

As well as PADI courses, boat and fishing trips, and snorkelling, Poseidon has a small museum showcasing artefacts retrieved from wrecks in the 1970s, and early Sri Lankan diving equipment.

ⓐ Galle Road ⓣ (091) 227 7294 ⓦ www.divingsrilanka.com
ⓔ info@divingsrilanka.com ⓛ 08.00–22.00

Splash Diving Center

A team of international diving instructors and UK qualified professional divers are on hand for dive excursions, training and courses. There is also snorkelling, boat rides, surfing and watersports.

ⓐ Coral Rock Hotel, 340 Galle Road ⓣ (091) 227 7021 ⓕ (091) 227 7521
ⓛ 08.30–16.00

▲ Hikkaduwa's palm tree-lined beach has a charm all of its own

TAKING A BREAK

Bars & cafés

Jah's Ark £ ❶ Quirky and cosy boat-shaped beach café with two tables, serving drinks and fruit. ⓐ On the beach ❶ No phone ⓛ 06.00–last customer, usually 02.00

Sunset Coffee Bar ££ ❷ This popular beachfront café attracts a good crowd, and is done up informally with flags and posters. It's perfect as a stop for fruit on the beach, but they also do main meals. ⓐ 348 Galle Road, on the beach ❶ (091) 438 3389 or 077 306 1068 ⓔ sanjeewa_sunsetbar@yahoo.com ⓛ 07.30–23.00

AFTER DARK

Restaurants

Blue Shadow ££ ❸ Blue Shadow serves snacks and main meals, including Italian, seafood and various heavily-spiced dishes. ⓐ On the beach ❶ No phone ⓛ 08.30–23.00

Coral Rock ££ ❹ Chinese, Italian and seafood are the main ideas at this big hotel dining hall, which has poolside tables. ⓐ Coral Rock Hotel, 340 Galle Road ❶ (091) 227 7021 or 077 791 1053 ❶ (091) 227 7521 ⓛ 07.00–21.30

Mama's ££ ❺ Big, slightly dark eatery with a bright mural to lighten the mood, and some fenced-off tables on the beach. You will find Chinese, Sri Lankan and seafood on the menu and the manager can also arrange diving, snorkelling and glass-bottomed boat trips. ⓐ 338 Galle Road ❶ (091) 567 7724 or 078 514 0805 ⓛ 06.30–22.30

Poseidon ££ ❻ Large, bright and airy eatery offering a mix of Sri Lankan and European fare. The food and service both come

recommended. ⓐ Galle Road ⓣ (091) 227 7294 ⓛ 07.30–22.00
ⓘ Accepts credit cards

Tigri ££ ❼　Mainly serving Italian and Sri Lankan dishes, this cheerful beachfront restaurant and pub is painted in bright blue and yellow, and has a few tables on a pleasant terrace overlooking the shore.
ⓐ 348/2 Galle Road, next to Sunset ⓣ (091) 490 3589
ⓛ 08.30–last customer

⬤ *You can choose your own fish straight from the day's catch*

Bentota

South of Beruwala, and nestling below the Bentota Ganga (river), Bentota is another popular package destination, but with a sprinkling of more high-end options. The river snakes southwards and then back west, meaning the resort is mostly bordered by water; perhaps one reason why the village remains relatively peaceful and undeveloped. The locals are friendly and eager to show you around.

But the quiet does not extend to the water: thanks to its calm lagoon, Beruwala is Sri Lanka's watersports centre, with various operators vying with each other to put you on a jet ski, in a diving suit, in a boat or on a surfboard. As well as adrenaline junkies, the resort appeals to package tourists with some spare cash to spend on their holiday, and also has a large German contingent.

BEACHES

Although Bentota is something of a package holiday centre, the beach is nothing like as cluttered as comparably popular resorts: trees, rather than beach shacks, line the sand. The northern part is known locally as Paradise Island, a thin strip of sand with the ocean one side and Bentota lagoon the other. This is a good starting point for watersports which use the lagoon. Going south, the sand widens out to become one of Sri Lanka's most attractive beaches, with overhanging palms that look too perfect to be real. The calm sea means swimming is generally safe.

THINGS TO SEE & DO

Aida Tours
One-stop-shop for your package needs, with cultural and nature tours along with meditation, Ayurveda and yoga.
ⓐ 12A Managala Mw ❶ (034) 227 1137 ⓦ www.aidaayurveda.com
ⓔ aida1@sltnet.lk ❶ 06.00–19.00

Club Inter Sport

Choose from wave-runners, wave-boards, waterskiing, banana-boating, jet-skiing or diving. If you don't want to get wet, they even offer some indoor sports. PADI instructors are on hand throughout the season.

ⓐ Bentota Beach Hotel, one minute from railway station
ⓣ (034) 227 5178 ⓔ bbh@keells.com

Confifi Marina

Snorkelling, waterskiing, windsurfing, deep-sea boat cruise, hobie cat sailing, catamaran rides, canoeing, banana-boat rides, river cruising, deep-sea fishing, and game fishing are all on the menu at this hotel-based operator. You can also take a PADI scuba-diving course, from beginner to dive master.

ⓐ Next to Club Bentota ⓣ (034) 558 1416 ⓦ www.confifihotels.net

ⓞ *Help conserve endangered sea turtles in Bentota*

River safari and other tours

Bentota lagoon is the culmination of Bentota Ganga, a popular spot for boat trips. Highlights include the birdwatching – herons, kingfishers and cormorants are usually out and about floating through the mangroves – and the Galapatha Vihara, a fascinating 12th-century temple in Bentota village. You'll also be able to do some shopping as you sail, as hawkers cruise up and down with their wares. They can be a nuisance, so beware. If you have the time, the river repays a longer trip, when you can reach remoter regions further upriver.

Sea Turtle Project

Doing its best to prevent the decline in Sri Lanka's marine sea turtles, the project buys turtle eggs, buries them in the sand while the babies develop, then nurtures them before releasing them into the sea. Visitors can participate in the process.

ⓐ On beach, north of Saman Villas, 3 km (2 miles) south of Bentota bridge ⓒ 08.00–18.00 ❶ Admission fee

Sunshine Water Sports Centre

Boasting Sri Lanka's top windsurfer and waterskiing champion on the team, Sunshine offers windsurfing, surfing, waterskiing, wakeboarding, bodyboarding, banana ride, tube ride, jet-skiing, deep-sea fishing, river-fishing, snorkelling, diving and river cruises from English-, German- and French-speaking instructors and guides.

ⓐ River Avenue, Aluthgama, north of Hemadam Guesthouse
ⓣ (034) 428 9379 or 077 794 1857 ⓔ funsurf@eureka.lk

Watersports

Most watersports happen in the resort's wave-free lagoon, and there's also a nearby wreck that's popular with divers. Snorkelling, waterskiing and jet-skiing, windsurfing, banana-boating, canoeing and fishing are all on the menu.

TAKING A BREAK

Restaurants

Susantha's £ Seafood and vegetarian options are both plentiful in this pleasant restaurant, set a little way back from the beach. Choose from over 380 items and dine in the delightful garden, whose trees, fairy lights and candlelit tables create a romantic atmosphere. Ayurvedic treatments are also on hand. ⓐ National Holiday Resort Road, Pitaramba, behind Bentota Police Station ⓣ (034) 227 5324 or 077 782 2044 ⓔ susanthas@sltnet.lk ⓛ 08.00–22.00

Aida £££ Well-arranged restaurant on the banks of Bentota Ganga. Around 100 seafood dishes are on offer, and the fish is fresh every day. You can also choose from more unusual treats such as Hungarian beef goulash and high-quality New World wines. The fountain and wooden roof complete the classy atmosphere. ⓐ 192 Galle Road ⓣ (034) 227 5398 or 072 353 4790 ⓔ aida1@sltnet.lk ⓛ 07.00–last customer

AFTER DARK

Nightlife

Wunderbar ££ The only disco in Bentota plays reggae, calypso, bongos and dance music until you're partied out, and the fun sometimes spills over onto the beach. ⓐ Wunderbar Beach Club Hotel, Robolgoda, 1 km (²/₃ mile) to the south of the main resort ⓣ (034) 227 5908 ⓦ www.hotel-wunderbar.com ⓔ wunderbar@sltnet.lk ⓛ 06.00–24.00

● *Storks and painted storks at Yala National Park*

Between Colombo and Kandy

Whether travelling by train or by car, the journey from the Sri Lankan capital to Kandy, the capital of the Hill Country, is a spectacular one, tracing the slow metamorphosis from hot, dry beach resorts to the lush mountain region. Colombo and Kandy are key points on the tourist trail, and the 100-km (62-mile) road between them boasts one of the island's main attractions – provided you like elephants – the Pinnawela Elephant Orphanage, and the nearby Millennium Elephant Foundation.

THINGS TO SEE & DO

Millennium Elephant Foundation

This home for retired elephants offers elephant bathing, fairly pricey rides around the nearby estate, a fun museum with enormous bones and primary-school type displays, plus the opportunity to sponsor one of the residents for a year, or even for life. Staff are on hand to answer any questions you may have of an elephantine nature.

The foundation is approximately 3 km (2 miles) from Pinnawela Elephant Orphanage, back in the direction of Kandy.

ⓐ Randeniya, Hiriwaduna, Kegalle ❶ (035) 226 5377 ❶ (035) 226 6572 ⓦ www.eureka.lk/elefound ⓔ elefound@sltnet.lk ❶ 07.00–17.00 ❶ Admission fee. Accepts credit cards

Pinnawela Elephant Orphanage

One of the highlights of a trip to Sri Lanka, the orphanage not only offers visitors a rare chance to get so close to so many animals (over 70 at last count), but has the added 'ahhh' factor that many of the residents were rescued from abandonment or injury. The babies are particularly winsome. Good times to visit are 09.15, 13.15 and 17.00, when the elephants are fed, and from 10.00–12.00 and 14.00–16.00, when they are moved over the road for a bath in the river. The site also has a shop, whose most unorthodox souvenir has to be pachyderm paper – posh stationery made from fibre-rich elephant dung.

To get there, turn off at the 82-km post on the Colombo-Kandy road. The orphanage is 10 km (6 miles) from Kegalle. The nearest railway station, 2 km (1¼ miles) away, is Rambukkana.

ⓘ (035) 226 6116 or (011) 271 7913 Ⓦ A useful website is: www.luckysama.de Ⓛ 08.30–18.00 ❶ Admission fee

TAKING A BREAK

Bars & cafés
Elephant House ££ It has fewer main dishes than its competitor Pinnalanda, and is not quite as well situated, but Elephant House is still a decent place to sit and watch the residents go about their business, and the staff are amiable. Ⓛ 08.30–22.00

Pinnalanda Restaurant ££ Structured to have several open balconies overlooking the river, Pinnalanda affords good views of the animals, but as a result gets busy and service, though friendly, can be slow. A nice place for a lazy meal, but don't expect fabulous food at this well-positioned tourist eatery. ⓐ Pinnawala, Rambukkana ⓘ 09435 226 5297 Ⓛ 07.00–22.00

🔺 Elephants bathing at the Millennium Elephant Foundation

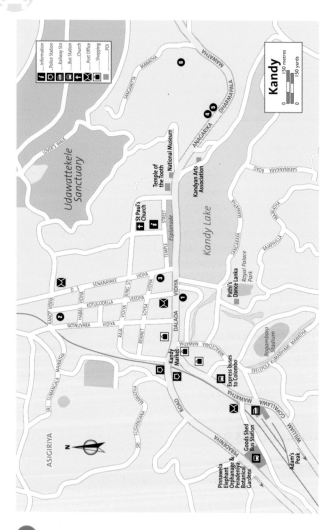

Kandy

0 — 150 metres
0 — 150 yards

Udawattekele Sanctuary

Temple of the Tooth

National Museum

St Paul's Church

Kandyan Arts Association

Esplanade

Kandy Lake

Pathi's Dance Lanka

Royal Palace Park

TEMPLE STREET

D.S. SENANAYAKE

KANDY VIDYA

KOTUGODELLA VIDIYA

HABAS VIDIYA

YATINUVARA VIDIYA

RAJA VIDIYA

VIDIYA

VEEDIYA

KING ST.

SOYSA

BENNET

DALADA VIDIYA

MAKADURA MAWATHA

Bogambara Stadium

ERELEDOLA KUMARIHAMI MAWATHA

Kandy Market

Express buses to Colombo

GOPALLAWA MAWATHA

WILLIAM

Adam's Peak

Goods Shed Bus Station

DEVADENIYA ROAD

SRI SUMANGALA MAWATHA

SRI TUSHITARAMA

ASIGIRIYA

N

SAKKAMITTA MAWATHA

DHARMAPALA MAWATHA

ANAGARIKA

SARANANKARA ROAD

SANGARAJA MAWATHA

RAJAPIHILLA

KUNDASALE

Pinnewela Elephant Orphanage & Peradeniya Botanical Gardens

Information
Police Station
Railway Stn
Bus Station
Church
Post Office
Shopping

Kandy

Kandy is the kind of city that seems more like a different country altogether than another stop on the tourist trail. Its uniqueness stems mainly from two reasons. The first is historical: thanks to its remote position, Kandy resisted European invaders for over two centuries – far longer than more exposed locations – and has retained a pure Sri Lankan quality. The second reason is meteorological: the cool, moist climate has resulted in lush vegetation that comes as a welcome and picturesque relief after scorching days at the beach, of which the town's Peradeniya Botanical Gardens are the highlight. This moistness gives the town its somewhat mythical, mystical appearance – a mist often hangs over the town, lending it the aspect of a lost kingdom. In fact, it used to be a kingdom – Sri Lanka's last – before finally falling to the British in 1815.

The centrepiece of the laid-back city is Kandy Lake, whose charm belies the fact that it is in fact artificial, built two centuries ago. This didn't stop the town being nominated a World Heritage Site over 20 years ago. Today it's a busy town, brimming with tourists and traders traversing the narrow and colourful streets with their fruit stalls and tuk-tuks. But the industry never makes Kandy feel big and bland, perhaps because of the fascinating religious sites and celebrations the town is so famous for. The lack of competing Christian culture allowed Buddhism and Hinduism to flourish almost unchallenged, and many of the city's top attractions bear testament to this. Probably the most intoxicating of them all, if you happen to be visiting at the right time of year, is the legendary Esala Perahera festival, a ten-day spectacle of colourful commotion (see page 103).

THINGS TO SEE & DO

Kandyan Arts Association
Founded in 1882 to preserve Sri Lankan arts and crafts skills, the association is still going strong. Evening performances of traditional dancing and music, plate-spinning and impressive fire-walking are

all guaranteed at the most popular and big-bang show of its kind in the area.

ⓐ Southeast of the Temple of the Tooth 🕐 From 18.00 ❶ Admission fee

National Museum

Kandy's National Museum is well worth a look for the variety of intriguing objects on show. Charting life before the city succumbed to European invaders, the exhibits include everything from floating clocks to astrological equipment.

ⓐ Junction of Anagarika Dharmapala Mw and Dalada Vidiya
📞 (081) 222 3867 🕐 09.00–17.00 Tues–Sat, closed Sun, Mon & public holidays ❶ Admission fee

○ *Dancers at the Esala Perahera festival*

Pathi's Dance Lanka

Not quite as flashy as the Kandyan Arts Association's effort, Pathi's offers the same mixture of extravagant costumes and headdresses, enthusiastic drum beating, singing, leaping about and bagpipes, but in more intimate environs, resembling something like a school hall.

ⓐ YMBA Hall, 5 Rajapihilla Mw ❶ (081) 222 2324 ❶ From 17.45
❶ Admission fee

Peradeniya Botanical Gardens

Making the most of Kandy's climate, the lush Botanical Gardens, nearly 200 years old, are a delightful place to pass a few hours, perhaps even the whole day. The almost 150 acres are home to 10,000 trees, an orchid house, lake and flower garden, but the highlight is a huge Javan fig tree, whose labyrinthine roots spread over almost half an acre. Even if you don't know your orchid from your African violet, the site's wide open fields, regal walkways and elaborate displays reward the effort. A restaurant on the avenue that leads in from the entrance shares its space with a shop selling dresses and sarongs. It's not the cheapest eatery, but the outside tables offer a wonderful view while you eat. The other option for refreshments is an ice cream kiosk near the entrance.

ⓐ 6 km (4 miles) from the centre of Kandy ❶ (081) 567 5357
❶ 07.30–17.45 ❶ Admission fee

Sri Dalada Maligawa (Temple of the Tooth)

One of the most sacred places, not just in Sri Lanka but in the Buddhist world, is the Temple of the Tooth, which for over four centuries has housed the Buddha's tooth relic. It's a fascinating, atmospheric site, with various rooms, shrines and a museum. Drummers and musicians playing a kind of bagpipes bang and play away, while tourists and worshippers mill around. The gleaming place is full of brightly coloured carvings, flowers, elephants, tusks and incense. There's also a stylish museum with black and white marble. If you can, time your visit to coincide with a *puja* (a service), which takes place from 05.30–07.00, 09.30–11.00 and

◔ *The colourful Peradeniya Botanical Gardens*

18.30–20.00. Foreigners are separated from locals, and all get to shuffle past for a glimpse of the casket that contains the tooth. You must leave your shoes outside, and short trousers, miniskirts and revealing tops are not allowed – you can buy a sarong over the road if you've come wearing the wrong stuff.

ⓐ Junction of Anagarika Dharmapala Mw and Dalada Vidiya
ⓦ www.maligawa.pooranee.lk ⓔ info@sridaladamaligawa.lk
🕒 06.00–20.00 ❶ Admission fee

TAKING A BREAK

Bars & cafés
If you're after a daytime sit-down and light bite to eat, try the town centre, particularly along Dalada Vidiya, where Kandy's many bakeries – too small and numerous to list here – are clustered. Selling what the locals call 'short eats', you can pick up local cakes, sweets and savoury snacks at bargain prices.

AFTER DARK

Restaurants
Devon £ ❶ Cheap and cheerful Sri Lankan eatery that has won fans for its on-site bakery. It also has some Western standard foods like steak and chips. ⓐ 11 Dalada Vidiya 📞 (081) 222 4537 🕒 10.00–22.00

Flower Song £ ❷ Highly-rated Chinese cuisine with a few Thai and Vietnamese options. Vegetarians are well catered for too.
ⓐ 137 Kotugodella Vidiya, Kandy 📞 (081) 222 9191 🕒 10.00–22.00

Rams £ ❸ If you don't mind the kitsch, slightly garish décor – and the lack of alcohol – the south Indian food on offer comes highly recommended – and cheap. ⓐ 11 D S Senanayake Vidiya
📞 (081) 567 0313 🕒 10.00–22.00

Andre and Sophia's Pub ££ ❹ Adjoining the Bamboo Garden Chinese restaurant, the pub offers great views over the lake and a spirited atmosphere. ⓐ 29A Anagarika Dharmapala Mw ⓣ 077 798 9796 ⓛ 10.00–22.00

Bamboo Garden ££ ❺ Trumpeting itself as the only purveyor of authentic Chinese food in town, Bamboo Garden is decorated in a predictable red, with lanterns. The food is decent enough and the place can get up a lively atmosphere at times. ⓐ 29A Anagarika Dharmapala Mw ⓣ 077 798 9796 ⓛ 10.00–22.00

Thilanka ££ ❻ Unlike lesser Sri Lankan eateries which go by the rule that the more items on the menu, the better, Thilanka focuses on doing just a few dishes very well. The dining hall is stylishly done out in black and white, with funky coloured horse statues, and the mood is smooth with mellow music and some tables by the pool. Lambs, prawns and seafood are good choices. Monkeys can often be spotted outside in daylight hours. ⓐ Thilanka Hotel, 3 Sangamitta Mw ⓣ (081) 223 2429 ⓦ www.thilankahotel.com ⓛ 10.00–22.00

Adam's Peak

Combining Sri Lanka's natural beauty and diversity with its reverence for sacred myth is Adam's Peak. With its summit at 2,243 m (7,360 ft), the conical mount is not even the island's tallest, but the *Sri Pada*, or sacred footprint, at the peak is said to have been made by the Buddha himself, and as a result the mountain is now a big pilgrimage site. Most tourists who make the journey there are doing so to join the devout in the climb – a four-hour slog that most people time to arrive at the top and see the sun rise. The pilgrimage season runs from December or

⬤ *Adam's Peak is a Buddhist pilgrimage destination*

January to May, which is also when the weather is best and there's the least chance of cloud obscuring the view you've made all that effort to see. Some visitors do climb out of season, but there are no lights and the tea shops that line the route are closed. There's not much by way of tourist facilities around the peak, barring a local market selling provisions for the climb and religious kitsch.

Adam's Peak is in the middle of the central hills. Reaching the area by car involves turning off from the A7 and taking a winding and slightly unnerving mountainside road. In pilgrimage season, buses run from Colombo and Nuwara Eliya to Dalhousie, the nearest village. Out of season, you'll need to take a train or bus to Hatton and get on a bus from there.

⬤ *Pilgrims climb the steps at Adam's Peak in the strong morning light*

Kataragama

Right up there with Adam's Peak and the Temple of the Tooth in terms of Sri Lanka's holy sites is Kataragama. Something like the Sri Lankan equivalent of Jerusalem, Buddhists, Hindus, Muslims and Christians all endow the town with spiritual significance, and many of its attractions have a religious flavour. The best time to visit is for the striking and sometimes shocking Kataragama festival, held in July or August. But whatever time of the year you visit, you're likely to be able to witness some kind of absorbing religious ritual.

Besides its sacredness, Kataragama's other main tourist draw is as the nearest town to Yala National Park. But if you can spare the time, don't be tempted just to pass through: the town's lazy pace of life makes it a relaxing stopover point.

The town is over 20 km (12 miles) inland from Sri Lanka's south coast. To get there by car take the B53. If you're coming by public transport, the bus, which leaves frequently, takes around 40 minutes from Tissamaharama.

THINGS TO SEE & DO

Archaeological Museum
Small but intriguing facility focussing on religious artefacts from the island. If your travel around the rest of Sri Lanka has been limited you might enjoy the mock-ups of famous religious icons from elsewhere. Members of staff will do their best to give you a commentary.
ⓐ Next to Maha Devale ⓣ No phone ⓛ 08.30–17.00 Wed–Mon, closed Tues ⓘ Donation appreciated

Sacred Precinct
The attractive park to the north of Sellakataragama Road is considered holy territory, and you may see pilgrims washing themselves in the river before entering it. As well as plenty of shrines, the park is also home to the ul-Khizr mosque and Shiva kovil, or temple. But the main highlights

are the part-Buddhist, part-Hindu Maha Devale, intricately decorated with elephant and peacock images, and opposite it the Kataragama shrine, an equally ornate affair flanked by two other shrines. But the interest is as much in the social aspects as the architectural ones. At *puja* time, worshippers flock to the area to set fire to and smash coconuts and dance, a fascinating ritual that takes place at 19.00, with lower-key versions at 05.00 (except on Saturdays) and 10.30.

ⓐ North of Sellakataragama Road

TAKING A BREAK

Bars & cafés

Guesthouses are your best bet for light meals during the day here. Due to Kataragama's religiousness, there is not an extensive nightlife. The honourable exception is the bar at Petal (see below).

AFTER DARK

Restaurants

Unfortunately, all this spirituality has a flip side: religious doctrine bars the local restaurants from serving meat or fish, and many also desist from using dairy products, too.

Petal £££ Catering both for believers, with its vegetarian menu, and the less devout, with a standard gourmet menu, is this elegant hotel restaurant. Anyone who has had enough of the solemn and respectful behaviour required elsewhere in the town can let their hair down with some karaoke in the bar. ⓐ Rosen Hotel, 57 Detagamuwa
ⓣ (047) 223 6030 ⓦ www.rosenhotelsrilanka.com

Tissamaharama

The historical town of Tissamaharama is something of a mouthful even for Sri Lankans and is often shortened to Tissa. One of the oldest royal settlements, the town retains a sense of its grand history, with many sites of importance that distinguish it from the somewhat interchangeable beach towns. Its most distinctive feature is the white Santagiri *dagoba*, built over 2,000 years ago, one of a few throughout the town. A *dagoba* is a stone dome which enshrines religious relics or a king's remains.

Dating from about the same time is Tissa's other main attraction, the artificial Tissa Wewa lake, which serves as a recreational centre in the absence of a coastline – the town is several miles inland – and as fertile birdwatching territory.

Tissa's location, within close driving distance of several national parks, makes it a good base from where to head off for some nature-spotting while enjoying a historical town in the bargain. To reach it by car, take the A2 or B53.

⬤ *A monk walks alongside Tissa Wewa lake*

THINGS TO SEE & DO

Birdwatching

Tissa Wewa, Vikum Lodge and several other sites within walking distance of the town are great spots for twitchers, with herons, egrets, kingfishers, woodpeckers, bitterns, storks and cormorants being just a few of the many species that frequent the area.

Dagobas

Tissa has several eye-catching large Buddhist shrines worth visiting. Santagiri, Yatala and Menik *dagobas*, all very close to Tissa Wewa, are the most high profile. At the Yatala *dagoba* you'll find one of the island's oldest elephant walls, plus a small museum with a few archaeological finds, although its opening hours are somewhat random.

TAKING A BREAK

Bars & cafés

Tissamaharama does not boast a great range of cafés; for a daytime snack any of the hotel restaurants should suffice.

Priyankara ££ The bar at this hotel comes with a range of cocktails and foreign wines as well as a pool table. Traditional southern Sri Lankan food shares the menu with continental classics in the relaxed hotel restaurant. ⓐ Road to Kataragama ⓣ (047) 223 7206
ⓦ www.priyankarahotel.com ⓛ 11.00–22.00

AFTER DARK

Restaurants

Refresh £££ Part of a chain, Refresh is very highly reputed, with outside tables and an extensive menu, from which the fresh seafood is the most renowned. ⓐ On road next to Kataragama, next to Podi Hotel
ⓣ (047) 223 7357 ⓛ 11.00–22.00

Yala National Park

The world-renowned Yala National Park is Sri Lanka's most popular wildlife reserve. The park covers over 1,000 sq km (385 sq miles), but only about 20 per cent of it is accessible to the public; the rest is closed off to

◔ *Leopard-spotting at Yala National Park*

protect and encourage the animal population. Yala is not served by public transport and must be seen in a vehicle – you can hire a jeep from Tissa, which is about 20 km (12 miles) to the southwest. Top of the bill at the park are the leopards. Although they can be relatively shy of humans, your chances of spotting them are decent, particularly if you spend a day rather than half a day on safari, which will allow you to reach deeper into the zone. There are no such fears of not seeing any elephants, who are numerous. Other residents include langur monkeys, deer, sloth bear, sambur, wild boar, crocodiles and some 130 species of birds, including plenty of peacocks.

The wildlife is obviously Yala's biggest draw, but the area is also worthy of attention in itself. Lagoons, freshwater lakes, different kinds of forest, scrub and rock monoliths make it one of the most diverse pieces of terrain in the country. On top of that, dotted around is evidence of Yala's early human residents, in the form of the remains of early settlements and temples.

🕐 Open 16 Oct–31 Aug

YALA NATIONAL PARK VISITOR WARNING
Before visiting the area take advice on the latest security situation. After several serious incidents in 2007 and 2008, the British Foreign and Colonial Office advised against travel to Yala National Park.

▶ *Street life in Sri Lanka*

Food & drink

A plethora of foreign influences, in the form of traders, invaders, migrants and colonialists, means that Sri Lankan cuisine is far more than just a lesser-known take on the Indian gastronomy that has spread all over the world. Arabs, Malays and Indians – particularly southern Indians – have all left their imprint on the local food, and further-flung European nations such as the Dutch, Portuguese and English have also had an input. The foreign effect is evident not only in the actual ingredients used, but also in the cooking styles adopted and adapted.

SPICES

The island is famously synonymous with spices, which is what brought foreign merchants to the country in the first place. Do not assume that because you enjoy an Indian takeaway you can handle Sri Lankan levels of seasoning. The local food is typically hotter than you'd eat in the south of India. Fortunately, Sri Lankan restaurateurs realise that overseas visitors do not necessarily share their own tolerance of spice, so the versions of dishes you'll be served will have scaled-back seasoning.

RICE

There are nearly 20 different types in the country, which vary in shape, colour and smell. Yellow rice is for special occasions, while milk rice is considered a lucky meal with which to celebrate the start of the year, or even the start of a month. In Sri Lanka, the rice is not seen as an accompaniment or side dish – it is the main event. This is the case with the island's staple meal: rice and curry (never curry and rice). Here, this can come unexpectedly spicy, typically with chicken, fish or vegetables such as green beans served in a coconut milk-based sauce. The rice, boiled or sometimes fried, is cooked in coconut milk, and the meal will be accompanied by lentils and chutney, both of which can be very hot. Another accompaniment could be a *sambol*, an often hot mix of ingredients to combine with your main meal as a form of seasoning, that can contain coconut, onions, lime, red peppers, spices, salt and dried fish.

Mallung is similar and features shredded vegetables and dried shrimps. Poppadoms and pickles might also accompany rice and curry.

HOPPERS (*APPA*)

Hoppers are also a staple in Sri Lankan cuisine: a snack more common for breakfast or lunch than for dinner. A pancake-like food, hoppers are crispy at the edge and tender in the middle, often with added flavour in the form of eggs, milk, coconut or other sweeteners like yoghurt or honey. A shot of palm toddy is often sloshed into the batter for added kick. A spicy onion side dish sometimes accompanies the hoppers.

FRUIT

Thanks to the island's tropical climate, one thing you will find in abundance and at great value is fruit: mango, papaya, pineapple and passion fruit.

RESTAURANT ETIQUETTE

As in India, the local people eat with their right hands. However, they realise that foreigners generally don't, and all restaurants should provide cutlery. Sri Lanka rises and goes to sleep early, and if you head out very late hoping to eat you may be left hungry, since restaurants usually close around 22.00. Some also shut between the end of lunch, around 15.00, and the start of dinner, 18.00 or 19.00.

● *A variety of spices is used in Sri Lankan cooking*

Menu decoder

Because English was Sri Lanka's official language until 1957, it is still widely spoken, particularly in the coastal resorts and other towns whose economies rely heavily on tourism. But using a few words in the local tongue will be appreciated, and if you do intend to head off and do any eating or shopping in out-of-the-way places, such as village markets, a few food terms may be of use. Sinhala, also known as Sinhalese, is now the island's official language, and the one mainly spoken in the south and west, so the terms below are given in that tongue.

GENERAL FOODS

Ala Potato
Amba Mango
Annasi Pineapple
Baht Cooked rice
Batalumas Lamb
Bittaraya Egg
Elavelu Vegetables
Haatu Mushrooms
Harakmas Beef
Isso Prawns
Jambola Grapefruit
Kakuluvo Crab
Karat Carrot
Kesel Banana
Kukulmas Chicken
Lemon Lemon
Luunu Onion
Malu Fish
Malu miris Pepper
Paan Bread
Palatura Fruit
Pol Coconut
Saladha Salad
Thakkali Tomato
Uroomas Pork
Wel dodam Passion fruit

SPICES

Caradhamungu Cardamom
Gammiris Pepper
Inguru Ginger
Kaha Turmeric
Kottamalli Coriander
Kurundu Cinnamon
Miris Chilli
Vanila Vanilla

MAIN MEALS

Ambulthial Southern Sri Lankan delicacy of marinated tuna
Batalumas Seasoned lamb cooked in a rich curry sauce
Dhallo Squid rings in traditional thick sauce
Harakmas baduma Marinated beef, stir fried with onion, potato, green pepper and pineapple
Hiriani/biryani Long-grain rice

with onion, saffron, cloves, cardamom, cinnamon, ginger and rose water

Isso baduma Spicy stir fried prawn

Kiri malu Tuna cooked in traditional coconut sauce

Kukulmas maluwa Slow-cooked boneless chicken in a rich red curry sauce

Masala those Urid dhal pancake filled with potato and lentil served with coconut sambol

Masala wade Crispy dhal with spices served with coconut sambol

Miris malu Spicy fish curry with chilli

SNACKS AND SIDE DISHES

Brinal pahi Aubergine pickle

Hoppers Delicate pancakes of rice flour and coconut milk

Kiri bath Rice cooked in coconut milk

Kottu Pancake with vegetables, egg, sometimes meat and spices

Malu paan Yeast buns filled with fish curry

Mas paan Yeast buns filled with meat curry

Mulligatawny Mild soup with lamb and rice

Patties Crispy crescent-shaped pasty with vegetables or beef

Thosai Savoury pancake made of lightly-fermented rice flour

DESSERTS

Kiri pani Yoghurt served with palm treacle

Watalappan Coconut cream, jaggery and eggs with spices

DRINKS

Ay-is Ice
Beema Drink
Beer Beer
Isma Juice
Kiri Milk
Kopi Coffee
Te Tea
Vaturah Water
Wine Wine

USEFUL WORDS
AND PHRASES

Athurupasa Dessert
Dhawal kaema Lunch
Kamata Restaurant
Kanda Food
Karuna bila ganna Bring the bill, please
Mama elavalu vitaray kannay I'm vegetarian
Menu eka penvanna Bring the menu, please
Rae kaema Dinner
Udhae kaema Breakfast

Shopping

Colombo is undoubtedly Sri Lanka's top shopping city, with Kandy running a close second, particularly for handicrafts. The capital definitely has the biggest range of facilities, from posh, Western-style malls and stores, such as Odel, Cargill's and Majestic City, and the even more upmarket Crescat, catering to rich tourists and the city's chic set, to the street vendors and stalls of places like Fort Railway Station and Pettah, where you need a sharp eye and even sharper haggling skills.

Low prices and colourful local traditions combine to give visitors to Sri Lanka an array of budget-friendly souvenirs from which to choose. Among the most popular are handicrafts, with the brightly painted masks of the kinds used in previous centuries to try to cure illnesses, ward off the devil or appease the gods – a big tourist favourite. They vary dramatically in size and quality, and the fact that a mask appears an antique may not mean that it is; some are deliberately made to look older than they are. Elephant carvings are also popular, again these range from small wooden ones you can pop in your bag to huge stone works of art. Tourist money is also helping sustain the island's metalwork industry, and if you're after leather goods the hats and boots can be of a reasonable standard.

If your budget stretches further, gems are another classic Sri Lankan gift or souvenir; the island's jewel industry goes back centuries. You can pick up precious stones everywhere from posh, professional boutiques to street traders, but caution is advised: you don't want to pay out for some pretty pieces of coloured glass. Colombo's Fort district is home to the National Gem and Jewellery Authority, which can test whether your gem is what you've been told it is. For gold and silver items, try Sea Street in the Pettah district in Colombo.

As you might expect, much of the island's merchandise has a religious theme. The Buddha crops up repeatedly in carvings and posters, and Hinduism and Christianity also get a look-in. Another gift category is tea, the island's largest employer, giving work to a million people. If you're in the hill country, you can pick up tea directly from the plantation. It's easy

⬣ A typical street market in Sri Lanka

enough to find the island's Ceylon tea on sale elsewhere, particularly in Colombo. As well as the classic tea, whose blends are ranked depending on the elevation at which they grow, there is a variety of other flavours. The Sri Lanka Tea Board (www.pureceylontea.com) is a good source of more information, and also sells small quantities. Quirky books on aspects of Sri Lankan life are another good souvenir choice.

Low labour costs have made Sri Lanka something of a centre for textile production, and the island has plenty of factories charged with supplying garments for Western retailers. Sri Lanka is an ideal place to pick up cheap spares if you're running low on holiday clothes: with good bargaining you can get T-shirts very cheaply, although at such cheap prices expect some shrinkage on subsequent washes.

Use your discretion when deciding whether to haggle for your purchases. Some stores – the more official ones – have marked prices; at such places bargaining is not the norm, although it may be worth asking for a discount if you're buying a few items or something expensive. The lower you go in terms of formality, the more bargaining is acceptable and even essential. Bargain with a smile and don't take it too seriously – the sums involved are likely to be negligible to a Western wallet. The tendency to rip tourists off is not as bad in Sri Lanka as in many other Asian countries.

Sri Lanka has tourist-orientated outlets, luxurious shopping boutiques with plush carpets or marble floors, air-conditioning and ultra-deferential employees. They often go by the fallacious name of a 'museum'. If you find the hard sell – albeit a very polite, Sri Lankan hard sell – embarrassing, it's best to avoid going in in the first place. On the other hand, if you have plenty of spare cash and want to be sure your purchase is genuine, such established operations are less likely to palm you off with defective goods.

A final word of warning: the sale of coral and shells depletes the sea environment and is against Sri Lankan law; you face a large fine if caught trying to get anything like that out of the country. And if you've bought antiques – defined as anything over 50 years old – you'll need a licence.

Children

As well as the obvious distractions of just playing on the beach, there's much with which to entertain younger travellers in Sri Lanka. If you're based by the sea, many of the less extreme watersports are suitable for youngsters, and almost everyone can enjoy snorkelling and boat trips. As ever, check the operator's safety provisions before committing. Another of the island's big draws is its wildlife. Older children will appreciate a day at Yala National Park, where leopards, crocodiles and elephants can be seen. Younger ones may prefer the family-friendly Pinnawela Elephant Orphanage (see page 72). The adorable baby elephants here will go down particularly well.

⬥ *Monkeys at Yala National Park will delight children*

But aside from the big attractions and organised fun, there is plenty in Sri Lanka's everyday life that will delight children. A ride in a tuk-tuk is an adventure in itself. The island's religious sites and symbolism – enormous, colourful Buddhas, temples replete with their own in-house elephant and orange-clad monks – will seem a world away from the places of worship they're used to back home.

On the practical side, bringing very young children – especially babies – to Sri Lanka has its challenges. Apart from the heat, you may also face a lack of essentials, such as disposable nappies, once you head out of Colombo and Kandy. Some restaurants may lack a microwave to sterilise your baby bottle. Pavements – where they exist – are not pram-friendly, and nor is the local transport network, which can get unpleasantly crowded. If young children are in tow, it's probably best to hire a car and driver. Public breastfeeding is generally not done.

However, with some forward planning the majority of these difficulties can be surmounted. Food is not a problem, with many places offering child-pleasing Western dishes like pasta and omelettes, and hygiene standards are usually high in Sri Lankan eateries, although it goes without saying you must use your discretion. There are often discounts for children sharing a hotel room with their parents, and in some cases no charge at all. The low prices in general make the island a good-value choice for a family holiday and whatever small inconveniences, the never-ending succession of Sri Lankan smiles usually compensates for them.

Sports & activities

Even someone with the most minimal knowledge of Sri Lanka could probably hazard a guess that when it comes to sports, cricket rules. Whether you intend to or not, you're likely to encounter some cricket on your trip, most commonly in the impromptu games that spring up on the beach. Even if you're not a fan, attending a match can be great entertainment. Forget newly-pressed cricket whites, polite applause and breaking for tea – here matches often have a carnival atmosphere, with loud music, men on stilts, and a general party vibe. Colombo, Kandy and Galle usually host test matches.

Much of what's on offer in Sri Lanka is beach based. Bentota is one main watersports hub thanks to its lagoon, with jet-skiing, waterskiing, banana-boat trips, snorkelling and diving among the options; Hikkaduwa is another good base if watersports are your cup of tea. Bear in mind that some sea-based activities can be affected by the monsoon; the watersports season is typically from November to April.

● *Treat yourself to a relaxing Ayurveda treatment*

▲ A visit to the Pinnawela Elephant Orphanage is unforgettable

Though not quite as common, trekking, cycling, white-water rafting and horse riding are also possibilities. Another of the island's assets is its wildlife. With over a dozen national parks, supplemented by various protected areas, birdwatching sites and animal enclosures, natural world enthusiasts will be inundated with choices.

But if extreme sports and tracking beasts involve too much expenditure of energy, Sri Lanka also has a more relaxing range of pastimes. Most famous among them is Ayurveda, which is becoming increasingly popular with European tourists. Ayurvedic doctors do attempt to treat serious conditions, but the majority of holidaymakers are just after a bit of 'Ayurveda lite', massages, steam baths and similar indulgences that are unlikely to effect a health revolution in you, but are pleasantly soothing. Some Ayurveda outlets also offer yoga lessons, although they are not as ubiquitous as in India. Meditation courses are centred mostly around Kandy.

The island's history has been peppered with foreign influences that have left their mark, and it would be a shame to visit without experiencing some of Sri Lanka's subsequently vibrant cultural life. Colombo has several fascinating temples, museums and galleries to wander around (see page 15). The island's traditions, including folk dances, drumming, songs and various fire rituals, are showcased in places like Kandy. They can feel rather touristy, but the colour and dynamism of the shows are certainly impressive.

Festivals & events

JANUARY
Duruthu Perahera, Colombo

Begun in 1927, this festival sees hundreds of thousands of devotees, many dressed in white, flock to Colombo's Kelaniya Temple to commemorate the Buddha's first visit to Sri Lanka some two-and-a-half millennia ago. There are three lavish parades, complete with musicians, performers, cannon fire and snazzily-dressed elephants. The first is called *Udamalua Perahera*, the second *Pahathomaluwa Perahera*, and the third *Randoli Perahera*.

FEBRUARY 4
Navam Perahera (Independence Day), Colombo

The capital's top parade, Navam Perahera involves traditional music and dancing and over 100 elephants. The best of the action is around Independence Square and Parliament.

APRIL 13–14
New Year, Nationwide

A family-orientated festival that unites Buddhists and Hindus in common celebration. New Year traditions involve cleaning, lamp-lighting, drum-banging and milk rice baths in the home before the parties – and, importantly, the eating – get started. Games such as pillow-fighting often see the whole village joining in. You might also catch an elephant race.

MAY
Vesak, Nationwide

The Buddhist Festival of Light involves, as its name suggests, lantern and light displays at home and on the street, as well as mime shows and street theatre in the vicinity of various temples. Roadside kiosks hand out free food, while drivers decorate their buses and cars with streamers. Some restaurants desist from serving meat, fish and alcohol around this time.

JULY–AUGUST

Esala Perahera, Kandy

Probably the country's most vibrant festival, Esala Perahera is a 10-day extravaganza of fantastic costumes, folk and fire dances, music, acrobats and lavishly-clad elephants, centred on the parading of a replica of Kandy's sacred tooth relic. With a history dating back several millennia, the festival incorporates various intriguing rituals, including tree-planting and water-cutting, with swords and symbolism aplenty. Timed according to the lunar calendar, the festival takes place in late July or early August, with the exact date decided about three months in advance.

Ⓦ www.daladamaligawa.org

Kataragama

Not one for the squeamish, the two-week event in the holy town of Kataragama sees participants walking on hot coals, being submerged in water, and piercing and skewering themselves. Less horribly, there is also a flag-raising ceremony and various religious rituals including water-cutting.

Ⓦ www.kataragama.org

Vel, Colombo

The big Hindu festival Vel, meaning spear, kicks off with a bull-drawn chariot carrying a statue of the deity Lord Murugan through the capital, and continues with a vibrant procession with the usual quota of musicians and elephants, as well as snakes and umbrellas. It ends up at the temple at Bambalapitiya, where participants smash coconuts and burn incense. Festivities culminate in the return of the chariot, which is marked by a firework display.

OCTOBER–NOVEMBER

World Spice Festival, Colombo

Bringing together top chefs from Africa, Australia, China, India, Malaysia, Thailand and their local counterparts, the spice festival is made up of events throughout the capital's top hotels and restaurants, plus a spice night market on the banks of Beira Lake.

PUBLIC HOLIDAYS
Duruthu Poya Full moon day in January
Thai Pongol 14/15 January
Navam Poya Full moon day in February
Independence Day 4 February
Maha Sivaratri February/March
Medin Poya Full moon day in March
Bak Poya Full moon day in April
New Year 13/14 April
Good Friday Varies
Labour Day 1 May
Vesak Poya Full moon day in May
Poson Poya Full moon day in June
Esala Poya Full moon day in July
Nikini Poya Full moon day in August
Binara Poya Full moon day in September
Vap Poya Full moon day in October
Deepavali (Divali) October/November
Il Poya Full moon day in November
Unduvap Poya Full moon day in December
Christmas 25 December

⊙ *Send a postcard home*

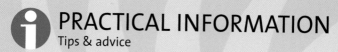

Accommodation

The following price guide is based on a double room with breakfast:
£ = less than R8,000   ££ = R8,000–13,000   £££ = over R13,000

BENTOTA

Bentota Beach Hotel ££ Reminiscent of a 17th-century Dutch fort
enjoying a unique beach and river location, this hotel has several
restaurants and bars, swimming pool, Ayurvedic centre and boat and
elephant rides on the beach. ⓐ Bentota ⓣ (034) 227 5176
ⓦ www.johnkeellshotels.com

COLOMBO

Cinnamon Grand Hotel £££ Luxury, comfort, space and a swish buzzy
ambience at this centrally located hotel. With 11 restaurants and bars, a
spa and swimming pool, plus free wi-fi access and 24-hour butler service
on the Executive Floors. ⓐ 77 Galle Road, Colombo 3 ⓣ (011) 243 7437
ⓦ www.cinnamonhotels.com

GALLE

Lady Hill Hotel ££ Originally built as a Church of England vicarage, this
hilltop hotel retains many of its original features and commands great
ocean views. Offers 20 rooms in a modern annex, pool, bar and restaurant.
ⓐ 29 Upper Dickson Road ⓣ (091) 224 4322 ⓦ www.ladyhillsl.com

HIKKADUWA

Amaya Reef ££ A beach setting, lovely lawned gardens, a pool, two bars,
a buffet restaurant and a host of activities and excursions make this a
good choice for couples and families. ⓐ 400 Galle Road ⓣ (091) 438 3244
ⓦ www.amayaresorts.com ⓔ amayareef@amayaresorts.com

MATARA

Sunil's Guest House £ Rebuilt following the 2004 tsunami, this friendly
guesthouse offers eight clean and comfortable rooms with some on the

beach. There's a pleasant garden area for eating. **ⓐ** Polhena
ⓣ (041) 222 1983, 077 742 4114 **ⓔ** sunilrestpolhena@yahoo.com

MIRISSA

Ocean Moon Cabanas £ Efficient family-run guesthouse, with 10 en suite cabanas in lovely garden setting with direct beach access. Fills fast so make early reservations. The owner can collect you from Weligama Station. **ⓐ** Udupilla Junction **ⓣ** (041) 225 2328 **ⓦ** www.mirissa.com

NEGOMBO

Ayurveda Pavilions £££ Well-appointed villa accommodation in enclosed courtyards, ideal for the truly health-conscious seeking Ayurvedic treatments, special diets and all the comforts of home. **ⓐ** Porutota Road, Ethukala **ⓣ** (031) 227 6719 or (031) 487 0765 **ⓦ** www.jetwinghotels.com

TANGALLA

Amanwella £££ An artistic combination of natural materials that blend seamlessly with the environment make this hedonistic hideaway perfect for special occasions. The elevated restaurant specialises in Asian and Mediterranean cuisine. **ⓐ** Bodhi Mawatha, Wella Mawatha, Godellawela **ⓣ** (047) 224 1333 **ⓦ** www.amanresorts.com/amanwella/home.aspx

UNAWATUNA

Thambapanni Retreat ££ A range of carefully designed villas, suites and bungalows set around a natural swimming pool. Ayurvedic treatments, yoga and meditation available. The restaurant serves a fusion of European and Asian cuisine based on Ayurvedic principles. **ⓐ** Yaddehimulla Road **ⓣ** (091) 223 4588 **ⓦ** www.thambapannileisure.com

WELIGAMA

Bay Beach £ Great ocean views from this modern 60-room hotel set in gorgeous gardens. Try fabric painting or cookery classes, enjoy sumptuous buffets or the à la carte coffee shop, or relax in the Ayurveda centre. **ⓐ** Kapparatota **ⓣ** (041) 225 0201 **ⓦ** www.baybeachhotel.com

Preparing to go

GETTING THERE

By Air

Unfortunately for anyone keen to minimise their carbon footprint, the only way to reach Sri Lanka is by plane. International flights arrive at Bandaranaike Airport (also referred to as Katunayake Airport), which is actually closer to Negombo than it is to the capital Colombo. The only carrier that currently runs direct flights from the UK is **Sri Lankan Airlines**. Flight time from Heathrow is between 10 and 12 hours. Several airlines, including **Qatar Airways**, **Emirates** and **Kuwait Airways**, do flights with a stopover at their home airport. You'll be lucky to pay much less than £500.

It's also possible to pick up direct flights with Sri Lankan Airlines from Paris or Frankfurt, and if you're coming to the country as part of a tour around Asia, there are good air links with most of the major hubs.

Many people are aware that air travel emits CO_2, which contributes to climate change. You may be interested in the possibility of lessening the environmental impact of your flight through the charity Climate Care, which offsets your CO_2 by funding environmental projects around the world. Visit Ⓦ www.climatecare.org

Sri Lankan Airlines
ⓐ Central House, 3 Lampton Road, Hounslow TW3 1HY ⓣ (020) 8538 2001
ⓕ (020) 8572 3808 Ⓦ www.srilankan.aero

Qatar Airways
ⓐ 7–8 Conduit Street, London, W1S 2XF ⓣ (020) 7449 6969
Ⓦ www.qatarairways.com

Emirates
ⓐ First Floor, Gloucester Park, 95 Cromwell Road, London SW7 4DL
ⓣ (020) 7808 0055 Ⓦ www.emirates.com

Kuwait Airways
ⓐ 16 Baker Street, London, W1U 3HS ⓣ (020) 7412 0006
Ⓦ www.kuwait-airways.com ⓔ lon@kuwaitairways.com

PACKAGE HOLIDAYS

Another option, if you're not planning on travelling outside Sri Lanka, is a flight plus accommodation package deal. Once something of an expensive and exotic destination, Sri Lanka is now in the holiday brochures of most major package holiday firms as well as some specialist ones. The prices of these can vary wildly, but if you find a good deal you shouldn't be paying that much more than for a scheduled flight.

Thomas Cook ❶ 0870 750 5711 Ⓦ www.thomascook.com

First Choice ❶ 0870 850 3999 Ⓦ www.firstchoice.co.uk
🕒 08.00–22.00 Mon–Fri, 09.00–20.00 Sat & Sun

Cosmos ❶ 0871 423 8568 Ⓦ www.cosmos.co.uk

Travel Sri Lanka ❶ 0208 099 9651 Ⓦ www.travelsrilanka.co.uk
🕒 Mon–Sat. Closed Sun

TOURISM AUTHORITY

The **Sri Lanka Tourist Board**'s official website has information on the country's attractions and the practicalities of planning your visit.

Ⓦ www.srilankatourism.org ⓔ info@srilankatourism.org

The board has several offshore offices:

UK & Ireland ⓐ 1 Devonshire Square, London, EC2M 4WD
❶ 0845 880 6333 ❶ 0845 880 6444 Ⓦ www.srilankatourism.org.uk
ⓔ info@srilankatourism.org.uk

TRAVEL INSURANCE

Taking out travel insurance is strongly recommended and inexpensive. The most basic packages start from around £1 (220 rupees) a day for a two-week or month-long break. For three months, expect to pay around £80 (17,000 rupees). However, essential-cover only packages exclude certain activities, and if you intend to go scuba-diving, trekking, windsurfing or similar, you may need to pay a bit more.

France Ⓐ 8 rue de Choiseul dans le 2ème arrondissement Ⓣ +33 01 42 604 999 Ⓕ +33 01 42 860 499 Ⓔ info@srilanka.fr

Germany Ⓐ Allerheiligentor 2–4, DE-60311 Frankfurt am Main Ⓣ + 49 6928 7734 Ⓕ +49 6928 8371 Ⓔ CTBFRA@T-online.de

Italy Ⓐ Via R. Morandi 3/E, 20090 Buccinasco, Milan Ⓣ +39 02 4570 5045 Ⓕ + 39 02 4570 9493 Ⓔ info@srilankatourism.it

Australia Ⓐ 29 Lonsdale Street, Braddon, ACT 2612 Ⓣ +61 262 306 002 Ⓕ + 61 262 306 066 Ⓦ www.srilankatourism.org Ⓔ kohinoorcentre@yahoo.com

The **Travel Sri Lanka** site is also a useful source of information on many aspects of travel in the country.
Ⓦ www.travelsrilanka.com

BEFORE YOU LEAVE

Doctors recommend the usual round of vaccinations for travellers to Sri Lanka: hepatitis A, typhoid, tetanus, diphtheria and polio. Depending on your precise plans – if you'll be spending time in rural areas or working in close contact with local people, for example – tuberculosis, meningitis, rabies and Japanese encephalitis may also be an idea. Much – but not all – of the coast where the main resorts are is malaria free, but if you're going outside of these areas you should consider taking malaria medication. Visit your doctor or a specialised travel clinic at least a month before your trip.

In the main cities and resorts you should be able to pick up most things that you've forgotten, but it's best to bring any prescription medications and possibly a first-aid kit with you, at least to save yourself the bother of having to hunt for a decent pharmacy. Sun cream, too, is a good idea – what's on offer in smaller towns is likely to be out of date. Women may also want to bring enough sanitary protection for the duration of the trip, as the local brands leave a lot to be desired.

ENTRY FORMALITIES

British, Irish, EU, US, Canadian, Australian, New Zealand and South African tourists require a 30-day visa, which is issued for free on arrival and cannot be extended. Your passport should be valid for an additional six months after your intended departure date.

🅐 3rd Floor, 41 Ananda Rajakaruna Mw Colombo ☎ (011) 532 9000
Check the department website 🅦 www.immigration.gov.lk
Customs rules allow you to bring in 2 litres of wine, 1.5 litres of spirits, and perfume for personal use. If you're staying in a private home, you should register at the local police station.

MONEY

Sri Lanka's currency is the rupee (known as LKR), not to be confused with the Indian rupee which is more valuable. One rupee is worth 100 cents. Coins come in denominations of 25 and 50 cents, one, two, five and ten rupees; notes in 10, 20, 50, 100, 200, 500, 1,000 and 2,000 rupees.

Banks are plentiful in the bigger towns, and you should also be able to find a bureau de change. If not, your hotel may well exchange your foreign currency, but the rate is not likely to be particularly competitive. It can work out slightly cheaper to swap traveller's cheques than cash. Whilst there are many ATMs, some only accept debit or local cards – check first.

The larger shops, stores, restaurants and hotels, particularly in the major towns, often accept credit cards, although there is a risk of fraud, and you may have more peace of mind if you take cash. On the coast, the devastation wrought by the tsunami means that many outlets, particularly diving centres, that once accepted credit cards currently do not – although some have reintroduced the facility.

CLIMATE

Thanks to the country's position close to the equator, temperatures in Sri Lanka vary little throughout the year: in Colombo the maximum average temperature peaks at 31°C (88°F) from February to May, then stays around 29°C for the rest of the year before creeping back up again in January. However, there is great variation within the island itself. While the coastal resorts in the south and west and low-lying places remain warm, temperatures drop in the higher parts where nights can be considerably colder. One thing that does remain fairly constant is the humidity – Sri Lanka's climate is tropical and it can feel sticky.

Another consideration, weatherwise, is the monsoon. The south and west coasts are affected from around April to October, with the worst of the rains in May and June. If you're planning to spend time in the main resorts, and perhaps head inland for some of the famous sights, January to April offers the best chance of minimising rain disruption, which can be a problem in the hill country. Going at the start of the year also means that temperatures have not yet hit their clammy peak.

BAGGAGE ALLOWANCE

Baggage restrictions vary between airlines. The best idea is to go to your airline or operator's website in advance, give them a call or check with your travel agent. As a rule, scheduled airlines usually offer higher baggage allowances than package tours. At the time of writing, Sri Lanka Airlines allow economy-class passengers 20 kg (44 lbs) of luggage in the hold and a carry-on piece of up to 7 kg (15 lbs), measuring 46 × 36 × 15 cm (18 × 14 × 6 inches).

During your stay

AIRPORTS

Bandaranaike Memorial International Airport, also known as Katunayake, is the country's only international airport. Located 35 km (22 miles) north of the capital, Colombo, and 10 km (6 miles) from Negombo, it is clean, modern and relatively efficient. You may find that your bags are quickly seized by an airport porter, but they are seldom aggressive and are unlikely to try to extort a ridiculous tip out of you. Facilities include a non-stop Sri Lanka Tourist Board booth, several competing small bank outlets that offer currency exchange at decent rates and car rental. You'll soon be surrounded by taxi drivers and touts, both official and unofficial. The licensed service charges a fixed rate which you pay upfront and you are then taken to the vehicle. Unofficial drivers are usually willing to negotiate and the journey can work out a fair bit cheaper, although this is not recommended. The journey to Colombo takes around an hour.

Another option is the bus, which leaves from outside the terminal to the left of the exit. It does take a bit longer, but it's a more colourful introduction to the country, and even if you are charged double for your

TELEPHONE CODES

To dial Sri Lanka from abroad, dial the international access code (00) followed by the country code (94). Then omit the first 'o' of the area code. When dialling abroad from Sri Lanka, the following codes are required (remembering to omit the first 'o' of the number):

+44 UK
+353 Ireland
+1 US
+1 Canada

+61 Australia
+64 New Zealand
+27 South Africa

bags it still costs next to nothing. Drop-off point is near the Fort Railway Station. There's also a train service that departs about 2 km from the airport (turn left out of the arrivals terminal) but you may have to wait over an hour before it comes.

If you're doing any plane travel within Sri Lanka, Ratmalana, previously Colombo's international airport, is now used for domestic flights. South of Colombo, it's close to Mount Lavinia, and is not served by public transport.

COMMUNICATIONS
Phones
Without a mobile, the easiest place to call abroad is from communications bureaux that you'll find in most towns – look for the IDD sign. Your call will be timed and you pay at the end. You can also pick up a phone card that can be inserted into private company payphones on the street. Some cybercafés, particularly in Colombo, also offer international calls via the internet. All options represent far better value than calling from your hotel, which can be exorbitant.

If you plan to send no more than the odd message home and keep in touch with your travel companions, texting from your mobile phone should suffice. If you're on a longer visit and are going to be relying more heavily on your mobile, it can work out cheaper to buy a local SIM card.

All telephone numbers in Sri Lanka should have a three-digit area code followed by a seven-digit personal number. If the number you're trying to reach is a digit short, try putting 2 at the beginning. If you have problems, dial 161 for local directory enquiries, 100 for the international operator or 134 for the international directory service.

Postal services
Letters and cards abroad usually reach their destination in a week or ten days, but two weeks is not unheard of. A postcard sent by airmail costs 15–17 rupees, a light letter 23–33. Surface mail is cheaper but less reliable. If you're sending bulkier items, they must be inspected beforehand, so there's no point wrapping them before you go to the post office.

If speed is of the essence, Sri Lankan Post offers a faster service called EMS, where items take two or three days to reach Europe, and five to seven to get to America or Australasia. Prices start from 1,200 to 1,350 rupees, depending on destination and weight. Post boxes are tall and red.

Internet access
Almost every resort now has internet access, although the expediency levels can vary: in Colombo you may be able to get online via your laptop in your hotel room; elsewhere you may be struggling on a slow connection in a cybercafé or communication bureau.

Language
Sri Lanka has two official languages. Sinhala is spoken by the majority of the population, with Sinhalese the main tongue in the south and west, the areas most popular with tourists. The island's Tamil speakers are concentrated in the north and east. Fortunately for the visitor, English is widely spoken and understood by both groups, particularly in the larger towns, and unless you go a long way off the beaten track it is highly unlikely you'll find yourself in a situation where you're unable to communicate.

CUSTOMS
Despite its relaxed and friendly atmosphere and eagerness to adapt for tourists, Sri Lanka remains a conservative country. Public displays of affection are not the norm, and young local couples making the most of time free from parental chaperones find discreet spots.

The rules are taken up a notch at religious sites, where you should be quiet and respectful, and never turn your back to a Buddha image for a photograph. It's usually better to ask before taking pictures in general. To greet a monk put your hands together as if praying and touch your fingers to your head, rather than offering to shake hands. Money may well not be openly solicited, but a small donation is appreciated – offering it with two hands indicates you are doing so freely.

Sri Lanka shares with India the infamous head wobble that can mean yes, no, or I don't know – and is virtually impossible for a foreigner to decipher. If the answer is important, try to get a verbal one. Another custom the country has in common with India is the use of the right hand to shake hands and eat – although foreigners' faux pas in such matters are usually overlooked.

In general, Sri Lankans are a courteous people, and it behoves the visitor to follow suit. Where local courtesy diverges from the Western concept is in the area of privacy: this is not a Sri Lankan value, and you will be repeatedly asked your name and nationality. If you're in the country for more than a few days, this can get enormously grating, but try to respond with good grace.

DRESS CODES

Flesh exposure is very un-Sri Lankan, although there is some leeway for tourists, particularly at and around the beach. At Buddhist and Hindu temples, your shoulders and legs should be covered, and you should also remove your shoes and hat. As in many Asian countries, the modest dress requirement applies in particular to women, and baring what is locally deemed as 'too much' can result in unwanted attention and hassles. Topless sunbathing is banned throughout the country.

ELECTRICITY

The electrical voltage is 230 volts AC, 50 Hz. Sockets usually take plugs with three round pins, although you may find the occasional one with square prongs or even two prongs. The oddities of the electrical system mean that some British and continental appliances work in the sockets. If your plug doesn't fit, it's fairly easy to find somewhere that stocks adaptors. Power cuts are relatively common.

EMERGENCIES

Most medical personnel speak English. If you fall ill, most major towns have hospitals. Colombo, of course, is the best served and also has a range of private medical facilities. If you're unsure where to go, ask your hotel receptionist or a taxi driver. Pharmacies are marked by a red cross on a white background. Even if you have health insurance, many Sri Lankan doctors, clinics and hospitals will ask for cash payment at the time, rather than claiming the cost directly through your insurance company. UK citizens with a valid European Health Insurance Card (EHIC) will receive reduced-cost or free medical treatment. You'll need to keep receipts for any treatment or medicines you've had, plus price tags and labels, to submit to your provider – in the event that these are lost or stolen you should report it to the local police station and get an official statement.

If you do require treatment, make sure you take your passport with you if possible. Other relevant documents, such as your driving licence and vaccination certificates, may also be worth taking.

Hospitals
Apollo Hospital ⓐ Kirula Road, Colombo 5 ⓣ (011) 453 0000
Asiri Hospitals Ltd ⓐ 181 Kirula Road, Colombo 5 ⓣ (011) 250 0608-11
General Hospital ⓐ Regent Street, Colombo 8 ⓣ (011) 269 1111
Nawaloka Hospital ⓐ 23 Sri Saugathodaya Mw, Slave Island, Colombo 2
ⓣ (011) 254 6258 or (011) 254 4444
Sri Jayawardenapura General Hospital ⓐ Kotte, near OCS and Parliament, 20–40 minute drive from Nugegoda, east Colombo
ⓣ (011) 286 3610–9

Policemen are a common sight in much of Sri Lanka; many, but not all, speak some English. There are tourist police units in the main tourist areas (ⓦ www.police.lk).

EMBASSIES & CONSULATES
British High Commission ⓐ 389 Bauddhaloka Mawatha, Colombo 7
ⓣ (011) 539 0639 ⓕ (011) 539 0694
ⓦ www.ukinsrilanka.fco.gov.uk
ⓔ colombo.general@fco.gov.uk ⓛ 08.00–12.30, 13.30–16.30 Mon–Thurs, 08.00–13.00 Fri

EMERGENCY NUMBERS

Emergency and Rescue Service 110
Fire Service 111
National Help Desk 118
Police Emergency Service 119
Police Emergency Service (from a mobile phone) 112

Canadian Consulate ⓐ 6 Gregory's Road, Cinnamon Gardens, Colombo 7
ⓣ (011) 522 6232 ⓔ clmbo@international.gc.ca ⓒ 08.00–16.35
Mon–Thurs
US Embassy Consular Section ⓐ 210 Galle Road, Colombo 3 ⓣ (011) 249
8500, (011) 249 8888 after hours emergencies ⓕ (011) 249 8500
ⓒ 08.00–12.00 Mon–Fri, closed Sat & Sun

GETTING AROUND
Car hire
Driving in Sri Lanka can be a little frightening, as the roads are very busy and traffic can be unpredictable. A less terrifying option is to hire a car with a driver. Provided you shop around and negotiate, this can work out as quite good value, particularly as many tour operators who provide the service have deals with some of the better hotels, so you can get a posh room for a knockdown price. The main downside is that the tour operator and driver have their own agendas: the operator to send you to towns where he has agreements with hoteliers, and the driver to take you to shops and restaurants where he gets a bonus. If you're flexible, this might not matter, but if you have a fixed idea of where you want to go it can be tiresome, and traipsing round extortionate tourist emporia getting the hard sell can be tedious and embarrassing. Fortunately, the majority of drivers will respect your wishes if you tell them firmly what you want – and don't want – to do.

Bus

Buses, the main means of transport in Sri Lanka, can be a fun way to get around – provided your standards of comfort are not too exacting. In its favour, the system is comprehensive and superb value: a journey of a few hours is unlikely to cost more than about 200 rupees, even if you are charged for an extra ticket for your luggage. The negatives include the amount of passengers often crammed on board and most drivers' somewhat unorthodox concept of road safety: buses may slow down rather than stop for more passengers to board and the most improbable overtaking manoeuvres seem to be viewed as a personal challenge. The usual practice is to flag down the bus (if you're not getting on at the terminal) and pay the conductor after you board.

At the no-frills end of Sri Lankan buses are the CTB (Ceylon Transport Board) vehicles. Private buses may appear little better, but sometimes make fewer stops and so get you where you're going faster. Private mini-buses supply the supposedly luxury end of the market. They do have air-conditioning, but still can be crowded and uncomfortable.

Sri Lanka's National Transport Commission runs a hotline that is useful as a first port of call if you want information about local transport but aren't sure where to get it.

ⓣ (011) 259 5555 ⓦ www.ntc.gov.lk ⓔ hotline@ntc.gov.lk
ⓛ 07.30–17.30 working days

Information about public bus services is available from the main bus stand in Colombo ⓣ (011) 232 9604/5. For details of private services contact the relevant local bus station office.

Train

The country's train network is made up of nine lines in total, with the two main tourist routes running along the coast (from northern Puttalam right round to Matara) and through the hill country (from Colombo to Badulla via Adam's Peak and Kandy). If your time is limited forget the train service, which is slow and often beset by delays. But if you're not in a rush, train travel is worth one try if only for the glimpse of history it offers. The line is in a similar state to when it was built by

DRIVING RULES & CONDITIONS

Sri Lankans drive on the left. Aside from that, there are few rules in evidence on the country's chaotic roads. Cattle, dogs, cats, pedestrians and bus drivers are among the unpredictable elements that mean that few but the very bravest foreigners contemplate getting behind the wheel themselves. If you do decide to take the plunge, bringing an international licence will save you the considerable trouble of having to get a one-month government permit.

Speed limits are 35 mph (56 km/h) in built-up areas and 45 mph (75 km/h) between towns. To drive in Sri Lanka you must be at least 18 years old. The drink-driving limit is 0.08 per cent, the same as in the UK and US – though naturally it is strongly advisable not to drink alcohol when driving.

the British, starting from the 1860s, and the carriages include ones imported from Communist Romania. First-class, sleeper and observation cars are a few of the draws, and often require advance booking, which can be done at Colombo's Fort Railway Station. As with the buses, prices are rock bottom. While reports of trouble are very rare, lone women should try to avoid sitting in carriages with only male passengers.

The main station at Fort houses an information centre ☎ (011) 244 0048 🕐 09.00–17.00 Mon–Fri, 09.00–13.00 Sat, closed Sun

You can also get details about rail services from the railway office in Colombo ☎ (011) 243 4215 or check the train schedules on the tourist board site 🌐 www.srilankatourism.org

HEALTH, SAFETY & CRIME
Health
Sri Lanka's food and drink poses fewer potential health problems than might be expected. Nonetheless, drinking the tap water is not advisable,

and you would be wise to avoid having ice in your drinks. Only eating piping-hot food and steering clear of street stalls and undercooked fish or meat is also advisable. For the first few days it's a good idea to take it easy and be cautious in your menu choices while your body adjusts to the food.

Although many of the coastal resorts are not malarial, some are, and Sri Lankan mosquitoes also carry dengue fever and chikungunya fever, so it's important to try to avoid getting bitten by covering up in light-coloured, loose-fitting clothing after dark, using coils in your room and applying mosquito repellent to exposed skin at night. Some hotels have mosquito nets in their rooms; you can also purchase your own.

While medical provisions may seem slightly primitive to the tourist, the standard of care in the larger towns is decent – although if you're in a remote area it may be better to go to Colombo if you require treatment, if possible. The vast majority of Sri Lankan doctors speak English; indeed, many trained in the West. Healthcare costs are generally low, but can rise sharply with a serious illness or incident. Private hospitals too have higher charges.

Perhaps the biggest danger you're likely to meet is the traffic. Sri Lanka's road safety statistics make horrific reading. Take extra care when on the road – particularly as a pedestrian. If you're unsure about crossing the road, wait for some local people to do so and walk with them.

Safety & crime

Sri Lanka's incidences of terrorism are mostly confined to the north and east of the island. The resorts are safer than many other parts of Asia, although in 2007 and 2008 Colombo suffered terrorist attacks. It is recommended that you check the latest travel advice at ⓦ www.fco.gov.uk. Tourists are very seldom subject to violent crime – though female travellers should avoid walking alone in deserted areas at night. Theft, too, is relatively rare, although bear in mind that the country is very poor, and the presence of rich Westerners – if you can afford to fly there you're rich by Sri Lankan standards – causes obvious temptations. Make sure your possessions are secure, whether they're in your hotel room (many hotels have a safe), on the beach or on your person. As everywhere, always be particularly aware in crowded places like markets and on public transport.

More likely than outright crime is the plethora of petty scams, some of which are quite polished. Any approaches involving street-based charity collectors, sob stories, gems, elephant festivals or tsunami bereavement should make you think twice. Of course, many Sri Lankans were bereaved in the tsunami – it's important to balance the self-defensive cynicism with an openness to talking to the locals, most of whom are among the friendliest people you could hope to meet.

If you do need assistance, the police are rarely far away, recognisable by their khaki uniforms and guns. Dealing with them, however, can be hit and miss. While many are helpful and friendly, reporting a crime can be a laborious procedure.

MEDIA

Of Sri Lanka's five English-language newspapers, the *Daily News* Ⓦ www.dailynews.lk and *Sunday Observer* Ⓦ www.sundayobserver.lk are state owned, which has an obvious effect on their impartiality. Their private competitors are daily papers *The Island* Ⓦ www.island.lk and *Daily Mirror* Ⓦ www.dailymirror.lk and the *Sunday Times* Ⓦ www.sundaytimes.lk. If you're interested, it's best to get the paper in the morning, as they often sell out by the afternoon. They are on sale in kiosks and from street sellers.

On television, MTV (Maharaja Television, not the music channel) and TNL are private English-language stations, but plenty of others show programmes in English, some of which are broadcast with subtitles. Your choices on the radio are the state-run Sri Lanka Broadcasting Corporation's service, TNL Ⓦ www.tnlradio.com, Sun FM, Yes FM and Gold FM.

OPENING HOURS

Most shops in Sri Lanka adhere to the standard working week of Monday–Friday, 09.00–17.30 or 18.00, with reduced Saturday hours of 09.00–13.00. Banks typically open at 09.00 and can close any time from

PRACTICAL INFORMATION

13.00 to 17.30 Monday–Friday; some also operate on Saturday from
10.00–13.00. Offices keep similar hours but usually close for the
weekend. Post offices, the larger ones at least, usually have their
programme from 07.00–21.00 from Monday–Saturday. Attractions
vary, but the closed day for museums is usually Friday.

RELIGION

Over two thirds of Sri Lankans are Buddhists, and temples – from the
tiniest roadside shelter with its bell-shaped *dagoba* to the largest and
most elaborate edifices – will be one of your abiding memories of the
national architecture. Monks, shaven-headed and brightly-clad in
orange or red, are an eye-catching sight in the temple or on the street.

Hinduism is the dominant religion among the Tamils in the north
and east of the country, with its followers numbering about 15 per cent
of the population, and about half of that amount again is divided
between Christianity and Islam.

TIME DIFFERENCES

In April 2006, Sri Lankan time was controversially adjusted back by 30
minutes. The country is now 5.5 hours ahead of GMT, 4.5 ahead of much
of continental Europe, 10.5 hours ahead of EST, 13.5 ahead of PST, 5.5 hours
behind Sydney and 7.5 behind Auckland. Being so close to the equator, Sri
Lanka has no need for daylight saving, so time differences vary by one
hour – the figures given are for European and US winter.

TIPPING

Tipping can be a source of awkwardness for Western visitors to Sri Lanka,
where it is an intrinsic part of the culture. If your restaurant has added a
10 per cent service charge to the bill, which is common practice, no extra
gratuity is necessary; otherwise rounding up the bill or leaving a small
tip will be appreciated. 100 rupees is about right for hotel staff. If you've
been on tour in a private car, the driver should be happy with 1,000
rupees per passenger, perhaps more if the tour was long or the driver
went above and beyond in helping you.

TOILETS

While toilets in the main tourist locations are usually clean and Western style, if you venture off the beaten track you may find yourself confronted with a squat loo. It's worth carrying some toilet paper with you, because it is not commonly used by local people. It's not thought of as a necessity, and even in the better hotels you may have to ask for it, rather than find it in your bathroom by default.

TRAVELLERS WITH DISABILITIES

Poor pavements, chaotic traffic and scant awareness of disabled issues mean that travelling in Sri Lanka with a disability can be challenging. Even some of the top hotels fail to provide wheelchair ramps, although there are one-level guesthouses which may be accessible. On the positive side, people are often helpful, and the low costs mean that you can hire a private car and driver cheaply. Some private operators specialise in arranging tours for travellers with disabilities.

The following organisations offer advice to travellers with disabilities:

The Royal Association for Disability and Rehabilitation does not run an advice service for individuals, but there is some general information on travel and its website has a section on the news bulletin board on which the editor posts details of overseas travel services.

ⓐ 12 City Forum, 250 City Road, London, EC1V 8AF ⓣ (020) 7250 3222 ⓕ 0870 141 0337 ⓦ www.radar.org.uk ⓔ radar@radar.org.uk

Tourism for All has information packs on some of the most common tourist destinations.

ⓐ c/o Vitalise, Shap Road Industrial Estate, Shap Road, Kendal, Cumbria, LA9 6NZ ⓣ 0845 124 9971 ⓕ 01539 735567 ⓦ www.tourismforall.org.uk

ACKNOWLEDGEMENTS

The publishers would like to thank the following individuals and organisations for providing their copyright photographs for this book:

BigStockPhoto 23, 42; FLICKR/Jikido-san 81; Julie Crane 27, 66, 78, 89; Getty Images 82; Pictures Colour Library 54, 64, 100; Sri Lankan Tourist Board 8, 29, 55, 73, 76, 87, 91, 97, 99; Wikimedia Commons 10–11, 18, Sarvodaya Shramadana 33; World Pictures/Photoshot 1, 71, 95; all the rest Vasile Szakacs

Project editor: Catherine Burch
Layout: Donna Pedley
Proofreader: Frances Darby

Send your thoughts to
books@thomascook.com

- Found a beach bar, peaceful stretch of sand or must-see sight that we don't feature?

- Like to tip us off about any information that needs a little updating?

- Want to tell us what you love about this handy little guidebook and more importantly how we can make it even handier?

Then here's your chance to tell all! Send us ideas, discoveries and recommendations today and then look out for your valuable input in the next edition of this title.

Send an email to the above address or write to:
HotSpots Series Editor, Thomas Cook Publishing,
Thomas Cook Business Park, PO Box 227, Coningsby Road,
Peterborough PE3 8SB, UK